Britain in the Age of
Economic Management

J. F. Wright

Britain in the Age of Economic Management

An Economic History
since 1939

Oxford New York Toronto Melbourne

OXFORD UNIVERSITY PRESS

1979

Oxford University Press, Walton Street, Oxford OX2 6DP

OXFORD LONDON GLASGOW
NEW YORK TORONTO MELBOURNE WELLINGTON
KUALA LUMPUR SINGAPORE JAKARTA HONG KONG TOKYO
DELHI BOMBAY CALCUTTA MADRAS KARACHI
NAIROBI DAR ES SALAAM CAPE TOWN

British Library Cataloguing in Publication Data

Wright, J. F.
    Britain in the age of economic management. – (Opus).
    1. Great Britain – Economic conditions – 1918–1945
    2. Great Britain – Economic conditions – 1945–
    I. Title   II. Series
    330.9′41′085   HC256   79-40545

    ISBN 0-19-219148-9
    ISBN 0-19-289135-9 Pbk

*Printed in Great Britain by
Cox & Wyman Ltd., Reading*

Contents

List of figures and tables

Introduction

This book is intended to provide an outline of economic developments in the U.K. from just before the Second World War until the middle seventies. I have used an older term and called it an 'Economic History' rather than the now more usual 'History of the Economy' because I want to avoid two impressions. The first is of seeming to suggest that the subject matter is some underlying layer of fundamental reality to which economists have privileged access as physicists have to the atomic world. The second impression is of focusing on the problems of government; in the usage of the day 'the economy' is an entity, rather like an imperfectly domesticated animal, though usually depicted as a temperamental motor car, whose importance lies in the failure of government to control it. In this concern with economic management there is a danger of forgetting that changes in trade, in the economic activities of households, in methods of production and the nature of work, and changes in the way firms are financed and controlled are all matters of interest and importance in their own right. It would be perverse in looking at Britain in these years not to give prominence to the role played by government, particularly to its deliberate attempts to control the pace and nature of economic development. But even these matters need to be seen against the background of more spontaneous economic change. This necessity underlies the order of the chapters.

Most important changes in economic life form trends or gradual changes in trend. It would be less misleading to see economic history as devoid of precisely dateable events than to see it entirely composed of such apparently hard nuggets of fact. So priority has been given here to describing trends, and no attempt has been made to provide a systematic and detailed chronicle.

My approach depends to a great extent on the vastly improved stock of statistics that has been a by-product of government's continual attempt to improve its control of the economy. A good many statistics are cited in the book; and the first stage of my writing it was to immerse myself in all the relevant quantitative evidence I could find. On many matters such data provide incomparably more reliable evidence than the alternative source of individual anecdotes or impressions. Because it is gradual, most economic change is not noticed by contemporaries; and often what is noticed is noticed because it is not normal. This is not to claim, for one moment, that statistics in themselves are sufficient. Normally they are of limited accuracy; they are often incomplete because particular measurements were not made; and sometimes what statistical evidence is available does not measure what we are really interested in. But they do constitute a starting point from which questions can be asked and in relation to which other types of evidence may be fitted into place.

My approach also involves a certain amount of economic reasoning. This is partly because, as an economist, I believe that the hypotheses of economists have some use, if only to provide a standard of simple-minded consistency against which to set the complications of the world. But it is also because during the period under review economists came to exert a greater influence on governments and events, and consequently their thinking shows more prominently in history itself.

It is impossible for an Englishman writing during the crises of the seventies about the preceding forty years not to be concerned with discovering the antecedents of those crises and not to expect his readers to be concerned also. Perhaps more than ever before, current partisan controversy about the economic situation involves assertions about recent history; and I cannot avoid many judgements that coincide with one or other partisan position. I have thought it better to state a clear-cut position where I have come to particular conclusions; but I should acknowledge here that the scale and format of the book do not begin to permit adequate substantiation of many of the judgements made. For all those who rightly require more evidence, it can do little more than provide an agenda for further discussion.

In many places a somewhat sceptical view is taken about the fruitfulness of government economic management; and there is a danger that my necessary terseness will be mistaken for acerbity. By and large individual ministers and civil servants are (like those with whom I am proud briefly to have served at the Board of Trade) men of exceptional intelligence, industry, and integrity; and they are usually no more to blame for the sorry circumstances over which they frequently preside than officers who find themselves managing the retreat of an army that has been put into an impossible strategic position by over-concern to live up to the sanguine expectations of the general public.

The final draft of this book was completed between July and November 1978. There is no definite earlier terminal date for the period it covers. On the one hand, it would have been artificial deliberately to have created a short period to which no explicit reference could be made. On the other hand, changes in trend are matters of historical interpretation, not contemporary observation. They cannot be discerned with confidence for several years after they have occurred and then frequently only in the light of subsequent events: to attempt to pass judgement on the information available in 1978 about the most recent period is effectively to move from history into prophecy. Indeed there must be a great deal that is provisional about my interpretation of the whole period since 1970. In producing it I have felt like a painter trying to capture a landscape on a sunny day with clouds running across the sky, each casting its own particular shadows and giving a totally different significance to features both in the distance and near to.

I must express my gratitude to John Cordy and Andrew Schuller, who invited me to write this book; Keith Thomas, David Attwooll, and Judy Spours, who have received the final product; to Sir John Hicks, who encouraged me to accept the invitation; to Robin Matthews, who made available a draft of his own much more substantial work; to Sir Alec Cairncross, Roderick Martin, and Jean Wright, who have commented on earlier drafts.

J. F. Wright

Trinity College, Oxford, 1979

Glossary of commonly used terms

The following terms are used in several places in the book. For others, used less frequently, the reader is referred to G. Bannock, *A Dictionary of Economics* (Penguin, 1972).

National Income is the sum of the incomes, whether earnings or profits, derived from producing goods or supplying services; and is equal to the value of those goods and services. More precisely it is usually measured either as Gross Domestic Product (G.D.P.) or Gross National Product (G.N.P.)

Gross Domestic Product is the sum of all incomes earned within the jurisdiction of the U.K. It therefore includes the interest and profits of foreign companies in the U.K.; but it excludes the corresponding incomes of British companies in other countries. G.D.P. seems the appropriate concept if we are concerned with the scale of the British economy viewed as a productive machine.

Gross National Product, by contrast, which is confined to the incomes of British residents and British companies but includes their earnings overseas, seems more appropriate as a measure of income. Both G.D.P. and G.N.P. are 'gross', measured before allowance for the depreciation of the capital stock, because estimates of depreciation are necessarily based on conventions, and do not meaningfully vary in the short run.

The **growth** of G.D.P., and of other quantities, is frequently expressed in per cent per annum, to make it possible to compare the *rate* of growth in two periods of different length. The growth rates so stated are compounded annually and, over a period of several years, produce a larger increase than simple arithmetic might suggest. Thus an annual growth of 10 per cent causes a quantity to become 259 per cent of its original size at the end of ten years. Conversely, at a 10 per cent rate of growth a quantity requires only seven years to double in size.

The balance-of-payments Current Account is a classified statement of all international transactions involving the sale or purchase of goods and services, or receipts and payments of interest and dividends by British residents. The balance of such transactions is therefore an indication of the extent to which a country's overseas earnings are in balance with its expenditure; and also a measure of the extent to which there will be a need either to borrow or to make payment out of reserves. It is not a measure of either the profitability or the net advantage of the international transactions.

The terms of trade are the ratio (expressed as a percentage) between the price of the goods exported and the price of the goods imported by a country.

Price changes, particularly in an age of general inflation, make comparisons in terms of money values of the output of different years quite meaningless. Comparisons are therefore made in **real** terms by taking an average of the changes in the physical quantities of outputs between the years (the 'average' being a 'weighted average' to allow for the differences in the relative importance of the various outputs on which information is available). Similar procedures are used to measure real income, expenditure, exports, etc. Sometimes, particularly when referring to trade, such measures are called **volumes**.

Logically **deflation** should refer to the opposite of **inflation**: to prices falling. In practice it is used more widely to refer to any situation of depressed demand, particularly one induced by fiscal or monetary policy, whether or not prices actually fall.

A **devaluation** is an increase in the ratio at which one currency is exchanged for gold or for some other currency which is accepted as an international standard (for example, the dollar until 1970). It is commonly thought that this makes all the exports of the devaluing country cheaper by the same proportion — but this will only be so in so far as export prices are stated in terms of the home currency.

1 Britain in the world economy

In the half century before the First World War, two processes altered the position of Britain in the international economy. The first was the diffusion of technology, particularly of manufacturing technology, so that Britain lost the industrial pre-eminence in textiles, iron making, and engineering that had characterized the first hundred years after the Industrial Revolution. The development of industry in the U.S.A., Germany, and other European countries was primarily a natural consequence of the British example, which could be imitated and improved upon. It was assisted by governments creating barriers around their domestic markets by the levy of high import duties. These developments led to Britain's loss within a short period of a large share of the home markets of her new industrial rivals, and also a part of other markets, including the British home market itself. Nevertheless, though serious for particular sections of industry in particular periods, the effects of increased industrial competition were, for the economy as a whole, offset by the second process. This was the expansion of international trade made possible by the improvement of the steamship; the migration to relatively empty lands, which were opened up by the building of railways and developed as important food producers; and the beginning of the extraction in bulk of the vast mineral wealth of the non-European continents.

Expanding markets for British industrial goods were found in the rest of the world to replace markets lost in Europe and the U.S.A. British firms dominated both the building of steamships and their operation, while British (especially Welsh) steam-coal provided much of their fuel. British institutions earned increasing incomes by acting as bankers in the finance of trade and as suppliers of long-term finance for development. The increased earning power from all these visible and invisible exports was enhanced by the more favourable terms on which imported supplies of materials, particularly food, were obtained. Though decelerating industrial growth in the U.K. caused concern and there was a slackening in the growth of industrial employment, the quite rapidly growing population that remained in the U.K. was supported at a standard of living that increased over the period taken as a whole. There was also a sufficient surplus of export receipts over import payments to permit large investment overseas by British savers.

A measure of the U.K.'s increased international involvement is that in 1913 about 21 per cent of the incomes of United Kingdom nationals (Gross National Product — see Glossary) was derived from the export of goods and services, an insignificant change from the 20 per cent of 1870, while a further 8 per cent accrued as a return on the savings lent overseas. In manufacturing taken by itself perhaps 45 per cent of incomes came from exports; while in the Lancashire cotton industry the proportion may well have been as high as 80 per cent.

In the 1920s the advantages which participation in international trade had brought to Britain were reduced by a sharp decline in exports below their 1913 level. A further diffusion of technology brought a growth of industry behind the protective barriers created by import duties so that, in the world as a whole, trade grew less rapidly than production. British exports proved exceptionally vulnerable. The growth of cotton textile industries, notably in Japan, which became an important rival exporter, and also in other countries, displaced Lancashire's exports. The opening up of productive coal-fields overseas and the replacement of coal by oil as the fuel for ships halted and reversed the growth of coal exports. At the same time an attempt to maintain the international financial position of London in face of competition from New York and other centres led to an over-valuation of the pound after 1925, which both aggravated the depression of the staple exports and reduced the incentive to develop new products to compete with imports. By 1929 the export of goods and services contribution was significantly reduced to 16 per cent of the Gross National Product. But the main problem is not revealed by this statistic. An inability to adapt sufficiently quickly to absorb the labour displaced by the decline in exports led to a national waste of resources that weighed heavily in the balance against the advantages of cheap materials and food which participation in international trade continued to bring.

For the world as a whole the 1930s saw a prolonged and deep interruption of the previous long-term growth. A lack of demand was aggravated by trade warfare designed to protect domestic employment. By abandoning the Gold Standard in 1931 the U.K. suspended the priority given hitherto to maintenance of its international banking role (in so far as that was dependent on the gold convertibility of sterling) and its subsequent exchange rate policy showed a willingness to engage in 'beggar-my-neighbour' warfare to maintain demand for British products. In 1932 the tariff of import duties, which had hitherto been confined to particular goods (chemicals and motor cars), was extended to all manufactures. In part the measure was intended to provide bargaining counters that could be used subsequently in negotiations intended to revive trade. The effect of the duties was also modified by the almost simultaneous agreement, at Ottawa, for lower duties to be levied on trade within the Empire — Imperial Preference. But, since there were comparatively few manufacturing exporters within the Empire, the simple protective effect of the British tariff of 1932 was considerable. It was indeed larger than the nominal rates suggest. For example, the duty on paper and board was 20 per cent although wood pulp was free. Thus, if wood pulp accounted for about half the cost of paper, the effective advantage of the British manufacturer over the foreign supplier would have been as much as 40 per cent of the value added in the British paper mills; either his operating costs could be that much higher, or his production would be that much more profitable. Some of the effects of protection were immediately visible as underemployed industries like steel recaptured a share of the home market. In other cases, its full effects depended on the encouragement it gave to investment, and this process may have continued for many years. By 1937 imports took only 10 per cent of the home market for manufactures.

By 1938 the percentage of export income in G.N.P. had fallen to nine per cent (less than half its 1913 level). However, this was not entirely a fall 'permitted' either by greater self-sufficiency in manufactures or by the very favourable terms on which food and material imports were obtained in the 1930s. Exports had declined more rapidly than imports, so that the £100 million surplus of 1929 of income over expenditure became a deficit of £70 million in 1938. Coal and cotton exports continued their downward path towards vanishing point. The increased share of the home market, which protection gave to many newer industries, did not seem to have increased their competitive strength sufficiently to secure rapidly growing export markets.

Figure 1.1 World trade and output of manufactures

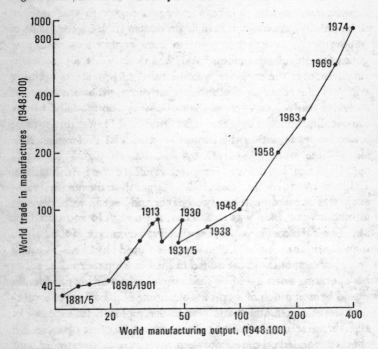

Note: Trade is measured by the total of manufactured exports. Both output and exports are measured in real terms. Sources; *United Nations Statistical Yearbook* and F. Hilgert: *Industrialization and Foreign Trade* (League of Nations, 1945)

The growth of world trade after 1948

Figure 1.1 is designed to compare the growth of trade with the growth of output of manufactures in the world; a line sloping at 45°

would represent a situation where trade was growing as fast as output. From 1913 to 1938 trade hardly increased, and even between 1938 and 1948 grew little. Thereafter for a quarter of a century it grew considerably (about eight times in 25 years) and more rapidly than manufacturing output (8·9 per cent p.a. compared with 5·45 per cent p.a. for 1948–74) though manufacturing itself had accelerated compared with 1913–48 (2·7 per cent p.a.). This long phase of rapid growth was interrupted, perhaps ended, in the middle seventies after the oil crisis of 1973; but it is worth noting that, even after rates of growth had fallen, trade continued to grow faster than output.

International agreements to reduce restrictions on trade and lower tariff barriers were important in permitting the relative growth of trade. During the Second World War and immediate post-war periods, disruption of their productive powers compelled many countries to restrict imports by quantitative controls. Subsequently there continued to be an imbalance ('the dollar gap') because of the surge forward in United States productivity, brought about by its wartime recovery from deep depression, which enabled it to meet an increased world demand for the type of goods which it was particularly experienced in producing. But although this delayed the effective operation of the International Monetary Fund (created by the Bretton Woods Conference of 1944, and designed to restore the multilateral basis of world trade which had broken down in the 1930s) and the General Agreement on Tariffs and Trade (G.A.T.T.) of 1947 it did not halt a process in which quotas on imports were made less restrictive. By the end of the fifties such quotas had virtually disappeared amongst the developed manufacturing nations and the process of tariff-reduction began. Cumulatively, in successive conferences under the auspices of G.A.T.T. between 1956 and 1966 (the Geneva Round 1956, the Dillon Round 1960, and the Kennedy Round 1966–7) significant reductions were made in tariffs by specific bargains between industrialized countries. And, at the same time, there were regional agreements (notably those creating the European Economic Community and the European Free Trade Area).

The role of these measures of trade liberalization was essentially permissive: they liberated powerful natural forces. Indeed liberalization itself would have been less likely if natural forces had been making for more sluggish growth. For then cases where individual industries in individual countries saw exceptional opportunities would have been more nearly matched by cases where other interests expected decline or increased competition and therefore sought protection.

There were several distinct factors making for growth in the relative importance of international trade. There were reductions in the cost of trade — partly in the cost of transportation in the simple sense of carrying a ton for a mile, but more importantly in the costs and ease of speedy communication with customers (telephone, teletype, and passenger plane) and of maintaining a quick and reliable supply of goods (freight-planes, roll-on/roll-off sea transport of goods vehicles). The optimum scale of production of many goods continued to increase, giving producers the incentive to look for overseas markets. Similarly the greater importance for producers of the costs of developing novel products and the accelerated pace of obsolescence made it important to sell goods more widely while their novelty commanded a premium. At the same time the rising income per head of consumers led to an increased variety of wants (and possibly an increased desire for exotic products), which it was difficult to reconcile with the need for standardization of output by domestic producers. Moreover the obtaining of economies of scale by more mechanized production itself created an increased demand for capital goods and, in many cases, required an increased variety of such goods.

One further factor in the relatively harmonious growth of the world economy needs mention. The growth of total manufacturing output, which itself accelerated, depended ultimately on the desire of consumers to spend a part of their additional income on manufactured goods — on road vehicles, television sets, consumer durables, and clothes. Without such buoyant demand there might have been more crises of over-production.

The process of diffusion of technology continued. Much of the flow was between countries that were already industrialized — particularly from the U.S.A. to Europe and Japan. While many less developed countries aspiring to industrialization proved inhospitable seed-beds, some, particularly in East Asia, achieved sufficiently high levels of efficiency for their low price of labour to offset whatever advantages earlier industrialized countries continued to possess. This sort of competition first emerged in textiles and clothing but spread in the sixties and seventies to the assembly of light electrical goods and even to shipbuilding and car production (in the case of South Korea). Such competition seemed most likely to occur where the industrialized process was relatively labour-intensive (a willingness of labour to utilize capital fully by continuous shift-work might effectively make apparently capital-intensive processes labour-intensive); and where the operation of the process did not require access to a wide variety of skills. Without continual innovation of new products commanding premiums for their novelty, and a capacity to switch resources into the production of these products, the older manufacturing countries would have been damaged by their newly industrialized competitors. As it was, in the case of cotton textiles from the early sixties, they did feel themselves damaged, and quotas and other restrictions were retained to protect domestic industries from precipitate decline.

The United Kingdom in the post-war world

Table 1.1 provides measures of the relative importance of different types of international transaction for the U.K. economy in the period since the War as compared with 1938.

Until the 1970s the net balance of current transactions was, taking five-year averages, no more than about half-a-percent either way — less than the adverse balance of 1938. At first sight this is inconsistent with the impression of continual balance-of-payments crises. What it does show is that the remedies adopted involved successful adjustment of the items of the current account to one another so that in the long run no net borrowing was necessary.

Throughout the whole post-war period the net inflow of interest and dividends was less than in 1938, and it continued to decline until the 1970s. The fall between the pre- and post-war periods was caused by the need to sell foreign investments to purchase war supplies between 1939 and 1945. Government expenditure overseas (particularly the maintenance of troops) was high in the post-war period and continued higher than in 1938. The balance of income from 'invisible' services (transport, tourism, and finance)

Table 1.1 Balance of Payments 1938 and 1946–75 (Percentages of G.D.P. at Market Prices)

		1938	1946/50	1951/5	1956/60	1961/5	1966/70	1971/5
Visible Trade	Exports	10·12	13·74	16·80	15·31	13·96	14·44	17·07
	Imports	−15·23	−15·14	−18·87	−15·71	−14·64	−15·11	−20·03
	Balance	− 5·11	− 1·40	− 1·93	− 0·40	− 0·68	− 0·68	− 2·96
Invisible Trade	Government	− 0·34	− 1·46	− 0·61	− 0·61	− 0·80	− 0·62	− 0·62
	Services	0·95	·48	1·10	0·83	0·70	1·19	1·60
	Interest and Dividends	3·45	1·88	1·49	1·10	1·17	0·98	1·27
	Balance	4·13	·91	1·93	1·15	0·61	1·00	1·77
Total Balance on Trade		− ·99	− 0·49	− 0·11	+ 0·60	− 0·07	+ 0·33	− 1·19
Private Capital			− 1·27	− 0·27	− 0·18	− 0·81	− 0·63	+ 0·65
Balance to be financed by borrowing or by loss of reserves			− 1·76	− 0·38	+ 0·42	− 0·88	− 0·30	− 0·54

Note: The table is intended to give an indication of the importance of different items of the balance-of-payments relative to the rest of the economy. To do this, the effects of the growth of the economy, both real and monetary, have to be removed by dividing by a scaling factor. For the comparison, very much the same impression would be given whichever measure of 'national income' were used.

Source: Central Statistical Office *United Kingdom Balance of Payments.*

was smaller than it had been in 1938, but subsequently recovered.

The net effect of the changes between the pre- and post-war periods was that visible exports and imports had to be brought more nearly into equality with one another. Imports were severely controlled until the early 1950s and controls were not removed until 1958. But in the post-war period most of the adjustment had to be made by exports, which by the early fifties had returned to a level of importance somewhat above that which they had had in the 1920s. The next fifteen years saw some decline until they started to increase again in the late sixties and early seventies. In this they continued to follow fairly closely the trend of imports, which despite the removal of controls in the 1950s fell from 19 to 15 per cent of G.D.P. because of changes in relative prices.

Figure 1.2 The Terms of Trade 1938–75

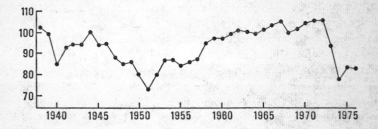

Figure 1.2 shows the movement from year to year in the price of exports relative to the price of imports, the terms of trade (see glossary). This ratio fell during the War and post-war period to about 75 per cent of its favourable pre-war level, the low point being reached in 1951 during the commodity boom associated with the Korean War. The next eleven years to 1962 saw almost as rapid a reversal, followed by ten years to 1972 on a plateau about the level of the late thirties. This was abruptly ended by a plunge in 1973 to about the 1951 level. The consequence of the long favourable movement in the terms of trade after 1951 was that the volume of imports was able to grow more quickly than G.D.P., although the import bill as a proportion of G.D.P. actually fell.

Table 1.2 Import Composition (Percentages of G.D.P. at market prices)

1938		1951	1956	1961	1966	1971	1976
8·1	Food	8·9	6·9	5·5	4·5	3·8	4·1
4·5	Materials	10·5	5·3	3·7	2·8	2·2	2·8
2·5	Semi Manufactures	4·4	3·2	3·6	3·9	4·5	6·6
1·2	Finished Manufactures	1·0	1·1	2·0	2·6	4·3	7·2
·9	Mineral Fuels	2·2	2·0	1·8	1·6	2·2	4·6

Imports

Table 1.2 shows the proportions of G.D.P. spent on the principal categories of imports. The declining importance of food imports was in part a consequence of the declining proportionate importance of food (in its 'raw' form) in family expenditure as real incomes increased. But it was also caused by the vastly increased production of British agriculture. The increase was assisted by government subsidies, but was primarily the consequence of the application of mechanical power and systematic scientific knowledge to most branches of agriculture. Similar factors operating elsewhere in the world produced a large fall in the relative price of foodstuffs after 1951. Expenditure on industrial materials fell despite a substitution of imported for domestic supplies of iron ore. In part this was due to a lower price of imports because of an increase of supply relative to demand and because of the reduction of shipping costs produced by the use of much larger bulk carriers. In part it was caused by the declining importance of the cotton and wool textile industries, which had been considerable users of imported materials; there and elsewhere there was also substitution of the synthetic products of the chemical industry for natural materials. Possibly, as well, it was a manifestation of a general tendency for the relative importance of material content in output to decline.

Most striking of all was the constant cost of mineral fuels (virtually entirely oil) despite the fact that in this period the relative use of oil as a source of energy rose from ten to fifty per cent of U.K. supplies. The main reason was the fall in the world price of oil in the fifties and sixties following the discovery of large cheaply accessible supplies in the Middle East and the desire of new countries and companies to capture part of the previously tightly controlled market. The money price of crude oil including transport to the U.K. was no higher in 1970 than it had been in 1948, though other prices on average had tripled. Other significant contributory factors were the fall in freights associated with the development of very large tankers; and a change in the location of refineries from the oil-fields to the consumer market. This was logical for the oil companies, both to remove their capital from regions where it was in danger of expropriation and to economize on transport costs by carrying unrefined oil in bulk and refining it nearer its final market. It was hastened in the U.K. by government persuasion and help. Its effect was to replace the previously imported services of overseas refineries; it also made available a large supply of low-value refinery by-products.

Imports of finished manufactures showed a rapid, possibly accelerating, increase; semi-finished manufactures also increased, though less rapidly. From year to year there were distinct spurts of import growth which tended to coincide with booms in the U.K.; but the increase continued in other years. This growth was to some considerable extent a consequence of world-wide liberalization which was increasing the importance of manufactured imports elsewhere. But the proportion of manufactured imports to G.D.P. was distinctly higher in the 1970s in the U.K. than in Germany or France. Since these are countries of similar size to the U.K. it might be expected that they would have had a similar need to specialize and import. The higher proportion of imports into the U.K. seems therefore to be an indicator of the relative failure of the U.K. industry to compete successfully in its home market.

Exports

As a result of the post-war 'Export Drive', exports of manufactures in 1950 were 60 per cent above their 1937 level, whereas manufacturing output in the U.K. had increased by only 34 per cent. In 1950, 25 per cent of the manufactures that were exported in the world came from the U.K. This was not so much higher than the 21 per cent of 1937, showing that, although the temporary disruption of Germany and Japan had created some opportunities, it was the expansion of world trade that provided most of the opportunity for the U.K. to increase exports. Subsequently the U.K.'s share of world trade in manufactures fell for quarter of a century to about 9 per cent where it levelled out in the mid-seventies. With the recovery of Germany and Japan a marked fall from the 25 per cent reached in 1950 was to be expected — but the extent and remarkable persistence of the fall marks a change in status of the U.K. in the world of trading countries.

The change in share of British exports does more than simply mirror the comparatively low growth of the U.K. economy in the fifties and sixties. For in 1951 to 1967 the rate of growth of U.K. manufacturing exports was only 2·4 per cent p.a. — distinctly less than the growth of manufacturing output, 3·0 per cent p.a.; elsewhere in the world trade was growing half as fast again as output.

There seems to have been a distinct change in this relationship after 1967 when U.K. exports started to grow more quickly than output. But it should be noticed that this change coincided with an accelerated growth of trade in the world as a whole, possibly produced by the tariff reductions, which also caused a growth in British imports of manufactures. Chart 1.3 therefore presents manufactured exports minus manufactured imports as a percentage of Gross Domestic Product. When presented in this form, 1967 does not have the same significance as a 'turning-point'; for the increased importance of exports after that date was offset by an increase in the proportionate importance of imports — particularly after 1971.

Figure 1.3 Manufactures, excess of exports over imports

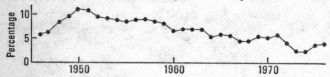

Note: Manufactures includes semi-manufactured goods. Imports are valued c.i.f. (cost, insurance, freight), that is, the price at which they are delivered to this country. Since they competed with home produced goods in this country this seems to be the relevant price; but the alternative, f.o.b. (free on board), that is, price supplied overseas, would simply increase the surplus shown in each year; it would not alter the direction of the changes shown.

After the resumption of export growth in the late sixties the relative importance of exporting in the economy increased to about 25 per cent of G.D.P. in the 1970s, while the proportion of the value added in manufacturing that was exported averaged 32 per cent —

probably not much less than it had been in 1913. However, the supplying of exports was a much more broad-based activity with many individual industries 30 to 50 per cent dependent on exports as contrasted with the exceptional dependence on exports of Lancashire cotton and Welsh coal in 1913.

Table 1.3 Composition of exports (percentages)

1938		1948	1959	1975
6·3	Chemicals	6·8	8·9	11·2
20·3	Textiles	19·5	7·4	3·6
12·4	Metals	12·0	13·3	9·5
25·2	Machinery & Vehicles	38·0	43·2	43·0
14·0	Other Manufactures	11·1	13·8	18·1
78·2	Total Manufactures	87·4	86·6	85·6
21·8	Non Manufactures	12·6	13·4	14·4

Note: An increasing proportion of exports have been unclassified and have been excluded from the denominator.

Over the whole period 1938–75 there were marked changes in the composition of exports: notably the decline of non-manufactures (mainly coal) and textiles; the growth between 1938 and 1948 of engineering and vehicles and its subsequent stabilization; a fairly continuous growth of chemicals; and, during the sixties, a growth of the miscellaneous 'other' category. The remaining coal trade was lost because coal production declined during the War and for fifteen years afterwards did not increase sufficiently to match rising home demand. Textiles flourished briefly during the post-war shortage, but thereafter resumed their decline. This was slowed in the 1950s and early 1960s by the development of synthetic fibres whose British producers initially preferred to supply local manufacturers, but subsequently competition from other fibre producers reduced this advantage. Chemicals grew in part because the U.K. was a convenient centre for processing imported oil and had, in contrast with earlier periods, a good supply of chemists; this capital intensive industry also benefitted from high investment incentives. But to some extent the growth in chemicals simply reflected their changed relative importance in world consumption, and the effect of economies of scale in making worthwhile extensive 'inter-trade' (that is, import and export by indus-

trial countries of different products of the same industry to one
another). One reason for the importance of engineering is, of
course, the wide range of products included under that heading;
but, if we are seeking to identify the elements of 'natural advantage', the importance of the U.K. as a supplier of engineering
products depended in part on the availability of a very wide range
of complementary skills, easily co-ordinated, with fairly considerable flexibility of output due to the concentration of a large part of
the British industry within a convenient area.

Table 1.4 Items of invisible trade (£ millions)

		Payments	Receipts	Balance
Sea Transport	1938	86	108	+ 22
	1954	484	520	+ 36
	1965	748	749	+ 1
	1975	2636	2648	+ 12
Civil Aviation	1954	38	38	—
	1965	134	162	+ 28
	1975	649	759	+ 110
Travel	1938	33	43	+ 10
	1954	101	95	− 6
	1965	290	193	− 97
	1975	875	1114	+ 239
Other Services	1938	14	35	+ 21
	1954	183	345	+ 162
	1965	311	594	+ 283
	1975	1347	2681	+1334
Interest Profit	1938	37	229	+ 192
and Dividends	1954	290	540	+ 250
	1965	557	992	+ 435
	1975	2006	2955	+ 949
All Invisibles	1938	206	436	+ 230
	1954	1398	1719	+ 321
	1965	2674	2871	+ 197
	1975	9507	11038	+1531

Invisible Trade

Table 1.4 gives an idea of the scale of the principal items that constitute the miscellaneous collection known as invisible trade. Taken by themselves the receipts constituted about 10 per cent of G.N.P. in both 1938 and 1975; but the surplus of receipts over payments which had been almost 5 per cent of G.N.P. in 1938 was only 1½ per cent in 1975 after having fallen much lower in the 1960s. The most important single items in this change are the flows of interest dividends and profits, where receipts grew less rapidly than G.N.P. because of wartime disposals of investments and the maintenance of controls on the outward flow of portfolio capital (that is, savers buying shares in overseas companies); and where an inflow of capital, as overseas firms invested in the U.K. and acquired U.K. companies, led to a subsequent outflow of dividends. In the accounts of dividends and profits there may be some spurious gains due to inflation and the depreciation of the pound which exaggerate the revival of invisibles between the mid-sixties and mid-seventies.

Turning to the non-financial invisibles we find that sea transport showed an even balance. Shipping is, in fact, very much an international activity, with many purchases overseas both of supplies and of ships themselves; and it does not fit easily into the conception of 'national' activities. What the statistic amounts to is that, by and large, British companies invested in a sufficient quantity of ships to carry the equivalent of Britain's own imports. Relative to many countries with smaller needs for shipping Britain remained an important shipping nation, but shipping was not as it had been, relative to other industries, an activity in which Britain distinctively specialized.

The positive balance in aircraft may reflect not only the considerable investment by the U.K. in her (predominantly nationalized) air lines, but also the geographical advantages of her situation in relation to Atlantic air-routes and the consequent revenue from airports.

Contrary to many predictions before devaluation in 1967, financial and other services prospered despite failure to maintain the international position of the pound sterling. This may well reflect the quality of the services provided by U.K. institutions: professional integrity, the wide range of complementary skills of the City of London, and the relative absence of bureaucratic and legalistic constraints. It was also the case that the same factors attracted foreign financial institutions to locate themselves in London, reinforcing the importance of the London markets. In part this may reflect the comparative attractiveness of London as a place to live for the employees of foreign financial institutions. But it also must have been affected by the low level of British costs: both in the costs of living in the U.K. and in the costs of British professional services.

A similar comment can be made about the 'balance of travel'. Up to the mid-sixties this showed a deficit, despite the constraint on personal expenditure of a limited allowance for overseas holiday travel. Subsequently it changed to a substantial surplus. This may reflect increased official attention to the 'industry' both in organizing publicity and in subsidizing hotel building. But it also depended on the relative cheapness of travel and catering services in the U.K.

This is a particular example of a more general economic phenomenon. Exchange rates have to depreciate because export industries lose their cost competitiveness — either because the productivity of these industries is not keeping pace with their overseas rivals or because workers in these industries force up their money wages relative to their productivity. The depreciation of exchange rates tends to offset this loss of competitiveness, but it is not necessary for it to do so completely if it increases the attractiveness of the output of other sectors to overseas customers. This can happen if there are such other sectors in which either the productivity gap is narrower (more precisely, has widened less) or the employees have been less successful in forcing up money wages. The relative 'cheapness' of Britain in the 1970s for tourists and foreign businessmen may therefore have been no more than a reflection of the low level of her industrial productivity relative to her industrial wage rates.

General Reflections

To some considerable extent Britain's nineteenth-century position had depended on her coal supplies. The importance of this, as a factor of comparative advantage, had been steadily eroded because of the opening up of supplies overseas — and by the exhaustion of Britain's own more accessible and richer seams. After 1945 it was nullified by the world-wide availability of cheap oil.

It would be an exaggeration to say that this left Britain completely without any naturally-based comparative advantage until the discovery of North Sea oil. Her geographical position on international trade routes, her natural harbours, her self-cleansing estuaries, the fertility of her soils, the variety of her non-metallic minerals were all of some value and were indeed the basis of many thriving exporting enterprises. Nevertheless, it is not misleading to say that the U.K.'s international position depended primarily on her competitiveness in manufacturing processes.

When trade is not related to natural advantages, the relatively low levels of cost of successful specialist producers are determined by the productivity of labour relative to the level of real wages. This is partly a matter of the effort and skill supplied by the individual workers, but it is also largely determined by their good fortune in working in locations where others possess complementary skills, including the organizational skills of management, or in locations where the industry has been sufficiently long established to reap economies of large-scale production. There will be other cases where the specialization depends not so much on relative efficiency in production as on distinctive products that command a premium over substitute goods. Such premiums may be largely or entirely dependent on the rare skills of the labour force, but in other cases they are attributable to the ingenuity and enterprise of managers. Two features need emphasizing: the pattern of trade is based on *relative* advantages; and the relative advantages that exist in one period are not immutable. The most fortunate conjunction for a producing country is to have products whose distinctive features command premiums over substitutes, and for it to find economies of scale in production. But new goods are devised and older products cease to command premiums. And, where knowledge of production techniques is common to all producers, economies of scale are passed on by competition to the consumers of goods leaving no special advantages to the producers.

Some set-back was to be expected after the post-war period. Then the British economy had enjoyed a brief respite from the competition of some of its industrial rivals, notably Germany and Japan; and, in the immediate post-war period, pent-up demand from the War even brought brief revival to the cotton industry. But, while U.K. industry had to expect to surrender some share of the world market, it was not at any positive disadvantage compared with its overseas rivals. Sometimes economists in their statistical analysis seem to suggest that there were such disadvantages, by the use of terms like 'structure of demand' or 'income elasticity' which seem to denote inherent natural qualities. Looking back on the period it undoubtedly is the case that British industry failed to gain as large a share of some of the most rapidly growing markets as did its foreign rivals, and that in aggregate the rate of growth of British exports was very distinctly lower than the rate of growth of the world economy. These were persistent relationships, and there must be a presumption that they were due to deep-seated causes. But the persistence gives us no reason to suppose that they were due to persistent causes outside the control of management, men, or government, rather than to persistent lack of management enterprise, labour inflexibility, and government incompetence. It is possible to argue that the U.K. in the twenties was 'structurally handicapped' in the sense that capital and labour had been committed to the 'wrong' industries in the previous period; but it is impossible to say this about the U.K. after 1945.

Geographically, the traditional distribution of British exports was favourable in the immediate post-war period when the favourable terms of trade of the primary producers were boosting their purchasing power; and the distribution became unfavourable subsequently. However, we should not read too much into such propositions about the geographical 'structure' of trade. Though a decline in the purchasing power of traditional customers was a handicap in the short run, it was not an irremovable constraint. Moreover, it cannot account for the whole of the U.K.'s loss of share of trade, since even within the individual traditional markets there was a significant loss to rivals.

2 The growth of the economy: some statistical dimensions

This chapter is almost exclusively concerned with the growth of output of the U.K. as measured by statisticians; with the relation of this growth to the supply of labour and capital; and with the major changes in the distribution of labour and capital amongst the principal sectors of the economy. It is primarily a discussion of macroeconomic aggregates; that is, of Gross Domestic Product, of labour supply, and of capital stock. The confidence we can attach to the apparently precise measures of these aggregates is limited. It is limited by the availability of detailed information: the active concern of Government with controlling the economy produced an improvement in the quality of information in comparison with the period before 1938, but it remained subject to sizeable margins of error. More fundamentally, it is limited by the extent to which single numbers can be used to represent the size of collections of what are in fact very different kinds of output, labour, and capital. Nevertheless, the aggregates summarize what were very large quantities of detailed information covering the economic activity of most of the economy. They do provide prima facie indicators of changing trends within the period and of differences between the period and its predecessors.

Total output and output per head

Figure 2.1 shows that G.D.P. increased very sharply during the Second World War and had fallen almost as far by 1947. From 1947 the growth of G.D.P. was much smoother than in the inter-war period, and until 1975 no year showed more than a very slight absolute decline from the previous year. From the pre-war 'peak' of 1937 to the 'peak' of 1951, which marks the end of the post-war recovery, output grew by 25 per cent or 1·7 per cent p.a. In the next 22 years to 1973 it grew by 85 per cent, or 2·8 per cent p.a.

Figure 2.1 Growth of G.D.P. '

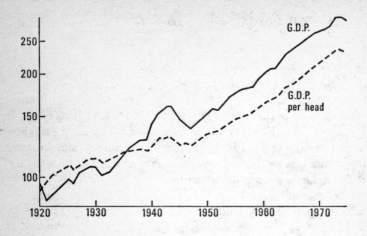

Note: Since the purpose of this graph is to show the *proportionate* rate of growth, its vertical axis is scaled logarithmically.

This is a distinctly faster rate than the 2·2 per cent p.a. of the inter-war period 1924–37, and, indeed, of any period after 1856.

The numbers in the labour force grew by 0·7 per cent p.a. between 1937 and 1951, by 0·6 per cent p.a. between 1951 and 1966, and declined by 0·4 per cent p.a. between 1966 and 1973, compared with a growth of 1·2 per cent p.a. between 1924 and 1937. Thus when we look at the G.D.P. per head of the occupied labour force in Chart 2·1, the growth between 1937 and 1951 is at a slightly lower rate than in the inter-war period (0·98 per cent p.a. against 1·04 per cent), while 1951–73 stands out still more (2·5 per cent p.a.). Within these years there appears to be some acceleration, with 1966–73 showing 3·3 per cent p.a. compared with 2·3 per cent p.a. for 1951–66.

If the rate of growth of labour productivity in the U.K. was so much higher than it had been in the previous hundred years, why was there so widespread a belief in its inadequacy? The main part of this question is considered in later chapters. Here we look at one particular aspect: the performance of other industrial economies.

Table 2.1 Growth of G.D.P. per employed person 1955–73

Rate of Growth (per cent p.a.)		1955-60	1960-64	1964-69	1969-73
U.K.		1·83	2·21	2·52	2·79
Five EEC members		4·53	5·15	5·29	4·63

G.D.P. per head (Italy 1973 = 100)	Belgium	France	Germany	Italy	Netherlands
in 1950	107	83	63	44	94
1973	141	132	129	100	154

Note: D. T. Jones: 'Output Employment and Labour Productivity in Europe since 1955' in *National Institute Economic Review* August 1976 (No. 77)

Table 2.1 compares the rate of growth of G.D.P. per employed person in the U.K. and in five E.E.C. countries (Belgium, France, Germany, Italy, Netherlands). It shows that the E.E.C. countries were growing about twice as fast throughout the period — although some narrowing of the gap in 1969–73 may be discerned as compared with 1955–60.

In itself the slower rate of growth of productivity in Britain than in Europe was no new thing. It could be seen in industry before 1913. What was especially significant about the period after 1950 was that the rate of growth of productivity in the U.K. should continue to be markedly less than that of the E.E.C. countries for many years after the *level* of productivity in most of those countries exceeded the level in the U.K. In a world in which knowledge of new techniques can be diffused rapidly, either as transmitted information or embodied in capital goods, thus opening up the possibility of simple imitation, it might be expected that any sizeable gap in productivity would tend to close itself by subsequent more rapid growth in the productivity of the low productivity countries. Indeed, such a process was almost certainly at work between the United States and much of the rest of the industrial world during this period, with the United States displaying a rate of growth much below that of other industrial countries though continuing to have a level of productivity much above theirs. That no such catching-up process was observable between the U.K. and Europe suggests that significant and persistent obstacles to industrial progress were operating in the U.K.

Table 2.2 Gross value added per employee in 1970 (U.K. = 100)

	Belgium	France	Germany	Italy	Nether-lands
Whole Economy	135	124	128	97	148
Manufacturing	155	164	155	105	183
Non-manufacturing	122	97	110	92	125

Table 2.2 shows that, in 1970, the differences in productivity between the United Kingdom and the E.E.C. countries were much greater in manufacturing than non-manufacturing.

The supply of labour

That the size of the labour force increased is at first sight surprising. The population in the working ages (15–65 for men, 15–60 for women) which had increased by 4·5 millions to 32·5 millions between 1921 and 1941 increased by less than one million to 33·2 in the next thirty years — mainly because the last of the large pre-1914 generations reached retiring age in the 1950s and 1960s. There was fairly heavy immigration in the 1940s with the settlement of refugees from Europe and the deliberate recruitment of immigrants from the Empire to fill vacancies in transport, the Health Service, and some parts of industry. Subsequently the inflow, particularly from the West Indies, India, and Pakistan became more spontaneous until curbed by the Commonwealth Immigration Acts of 1962 and 1968. It is less well known that this immigration was matched numerically by a continuous net emigration to Canada, Australasia, and South Africa.

One explanation for the increase in the labour force is the decline in unemployment. From 1945 until 1967 unemployment rarely exceeded ½ million, and was often very much lower, as compared with 1937 (itself a relatively good year) when there were nearly 1½ million unemployed. But this 'mopping up' of the unemployed was a 'once-for-all' factor. The explanation of the continued growth of the working population must lie in a net increase in 'participation': the willingness of the population to seek employment.

The explanation lies entirely in the increased participation in employment of women, particularly married women. Participation amongst other groups declined. Among the young the cause of decline was the extension of the school leaving age to 15 in 1947 and to 16 in 1972, augmented by a considerable increase in the numbers staying at school to 18 and then proceeding to several years of tertiary education. The elderly in the 1930s frequently remained in employment after the nominal retiring ages of 65 and 60; in 1938, 33 per cent were reported to be so. In the early 1950s the proportion again rose slightly, reaching 26 per cent in 1957, but fell away steadily thereafter to 17 per cent in the late sixties.

In 1931 women constituted 29·7 per cent of the labour force; in 1966 they constituted 35·7 per cent, despite the fact that the ratio of women to men in the working ages had declined from 1·03 to 0·91. Moreover in the same period the proportion of women getting married increased and the age of marriage fell — both factors which might have been expected to reduce the proportion of women working. Table 6.1 (page 91) shows that in 1931 only 10 per cent of married women of working age were employed. This proportion had increased to 20 per cent in 1951 and was about 50 per cent in 1971. Each age group showed an increase in each period, but the increase among the over 45s was especially marked. Among women over 30, 10 to 20 per cent more took employment than in Germany or France in 1975; only in Denmark was the proportion as high as in the U.K. That the increase in the labour force was coming from married women, and increasingly from older married women, is of some importance. Such labour was not very suitable to meet many of the shortages that occurred; in particular it was not available for work very far from home, and it was not available for heavy manual work.

The discussion so far is entirely in terms of numbers employed; and the measure of productivity is output per man year. But it is open to the individuals in a society to take some of the benefit of economic progress in the form of reduced hours of labour. Over the previous hundred years such reductions in hours had been an important enhancement of the benefits of the more visible increase in output per man year. During the post-war period the 'normal' working week fell from 44½ hours in 1951 to 40 in the early seventies. But this was of most significance as a basis for calculating overtime payments; 'actual' working hours fell in the same period from 47·8 in 1951 to 45·6 in 1973 (i.e. a fall of 4½ per cent); and, at this level, were 5 to 10 per cent longer than most other developed countries.

As important as the decline in hours was the lengthening of holidays, which probably on average at least doubled from two weeks to four weeks, a reduction in the working year of 5 per cent. It should be emphasized that these sketchy statistics are confined to manual workers. Nominal hours of work in many other occupations declined, particularly with the widespread abandonment of Saturday morning working: but where payment is not made by the hour there is no record of hours worked.

A 4½ per cent reduction in the working week and a 5 per cent reduction in the number of weeks in the working year produces an estimate of labour supply, measured in man-hours, that shows no growth between 1951 and 1964 and a decline thereafter. If this measure (rather than simple numbers in the labour force), is used as the denominator in calculating productivity, the acceleration in productivity is more marked from 0·7 per cent p.a. in 1924–37, to 1·7 per cent p.a. in 1937–51, to 2·9 per cent p.a. in 1951–64, and to 3·2 per cent p.a. in 1964–73.

Investment and the stock of capital

Figure 2.2 Gross Domestic Fixed Capital Formation as percentage of G.D.P.

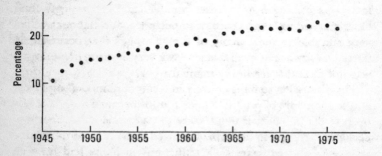

Investment had to be severely restrained during the War, and in the immediate post-war period was limited by the need to use engineering capacity to produce exports. Despite this limitation, 13·8 per cent of G.D.P. in 1948 was used for Gross Domestic Fixed Capital Formation (new houses and buildings, plant, and vehicles for business). The percentage reached 15 by 1950. Thereafter it rose more slowly; but it did rise with few and very minor setbacks until it reached 23 per cent in 1973. These percentages need to be compared with the 12·0 per cent of G.D.P. in 1938 — itself high compared with a more normal approximate 10 per cent earlier in the century.

These estimates of capital formation do not allow for 'capital consumption', that is, for the decline, through physical deterioration or technical obsolescence, of the capital already existing. Allowing for this 'capital consumption', the remaining 'net capital formation' in 1948 at 5·1 per cent was actually a little less than in 1938 (5·7 per cent) and there was a significant growth to 9 per cent in 1959 and 11·4 per cent in 1973.

Table 2.3 Capital stock at 1970 prices (thousand millions of pounds)

	1938	1948	1975
Railway Rolling Stock etc.,			
Road Vehicles	5·2	4·8	10·1
Plant/Machinery	13·4	15·7	48·5
Dwellings	20·2	21·3	42·7
Other Buildings	26·4	26·7	57·4

Table 2.3 presents the effect of investment in the form of estimates of the accumulated stock of capital in existence in 1938, 1948, and 1975 valued at 1970 prices. Over the whole period the stock of plant and machinery grew very much faster (nearly four times) than the other categories — though they themselves doubled.

Between 1937 and 1951 the amount of capital per worker employed grew very slowly (0· 22 per cent p.a.). It also grew more slowly than the growth of output — so that the capital-output ratio fell from 3·9 to 3·5. This trend was not a feature peculiar to Britain due to low wartime investment; it fell at least as much in other countries, including the U.S.A. Between 1951 and 1966, capital per employed worker was increasing at 2.3 per cent p.a. Since this is very much the same as the growth of output per worker it implies very little change in the capital-output ratio. After 1966 there was a perceptible change. The growth of capital per worker, 4·5 per cent p.a., was faster than the growth of output; and consequently the capital-output ratio rose again to 3·9 in 1974. From the ratio considered in isolation it is not possible to say whether the trend after 1966 reflects increasing inefficiency in the utilization of capital, or whether it reflects the end of an epoch in which technological change brought economies in capital as well as labour. There were similar trends in other countries. On the other hand, it must be noted that though the directions of change were similar, capital-output ratios in other countries were (in so far as the statistics are comparable) distinctly lower than in the U.K. — suggesting a more efficient use of capital overseas.

Total Factor Productivity

How far was the growth in output per unit of labour attributable to the growth in the amount of capital available to each unit of labour? Table 2.4 presents one type of calculation that gives a rough answer to that question. The first stage is to calculate the growth of labour and capital together, the 'weighted inputs'. (This is done by taking their growth rates and multiplying them by their shares in the G.D.P.) The difference between the actual rate of growth of output and the growth of inputs so calculated has been called Total Factor Productivity (T.F.P.). Essentially it is a measure of the unexplained residual of growth of output. We cannot say

Table 2.4 Growth of Output and Productivity 1924–73 (per cent p.a.)

	Output	Labour	Capital	Labour Productivity	Weighted Inputs	Weighted T.F.P.
1924–37	2·2	1·5	1·7	0·7	1·5	0·7
1937–51	1·8	0·1	1·1	1·7	0·4	1·4
1951–64	2·9	0·0	2·8	2·9	0·7	2·2
1964–73	2·7	−0·5	4·0	3·2	0·7	2·0

Source: R. C. O. Matthews and C. H. Feinstein (unpublished) for 1924–64. Author's rough estimates for 1964–73.

how far it is to be explained by other non-measured causes, or how far it might be explained by the possibility that the effect of factor inputs is not simply proportionate to their size, but has some ingredient of economies of scale. On this calculation the growth of T.F.P. rises from 0·7 per cent p.a. in the inter-war period to 1·4 per cent p.a. in 1937–51; still further to 2· 2 per cent for 1951–64; and then falls back slightly to 2· 0 per cent for 1964–73 — this latter being the counterpart of the increasing capital-output ratio of that period.

The principal sectors of the economy

Table 2.5 Percentage distribution of employed population

	1938	1948	1961	1974
Agriculture	5·1	4·3	3·2	1·8
Mining & Quarrying	4·7	4·0	3·3	1·6
Manufacture	33·3	36·8	38·4	34·6
of which Chemicals	*1·2*	*1·9*	*2·0*	*1·9*
Engineering	*9·9*	*13·7*	*13·9*	*13·1*
Textiles	*9·1*	*7·7*	*6·0*	*4·3*
Building & Contracting	6·0	6·4	6·6	5·8
Gas & Electricity	1·5	1·6	1·7	1·5
Transport & Communications	8·6	9·0	7·6	6·7
Distribution	14·4	11·1	12·4	12·1
Finance & Professional	8·7	10·0	12·6	19·7
Miscellaneous	15·1	9·8	8·2	9·4
Government	2·3	6·8	5·9	7·0

Note: The classification of industries was altered in 1948 and 1969; and this makes comparison of the original figures difficult. The percentages in Table 2.4 are the product of some rough calculations to try to avoid this difficulty — but they should not be used for any other purpose or without this warning.

The growth of the economy was accompanied by some changes in the relative importance of its different branches. Table 2.5 provides one type of indication of these changes — though it should be noted that in some very capital-intensive sectors like Chemicals or Electricity employment is likely to understate importance. (It should also be noted that because of changes in the methods of classifying employments the estimates are much less definite than might be expected.) The War produced an increase in the importance of manufacturing that was resumed in the 1950s; from the end of that decade, however, it started declining persistently. The share of G.D.P. contributed tells much the same tale, except that the increase from 1938–48 was half as large again. Transport and Distribution showed some decline in employment; but the most marked falls were in Agriculture, Mining, and 'Miscellaneous' (of which probably the largest part was the end of full-time domestic service). Financial and Professional employments, which included many public employees in the health and educational services, more than doubled.

Table 2.6 Sectoral growth in the U.K. (per cent p.a.)

	Output	Labour	Capital	Labour Prod.	T.F.P.
1924–37					
Agriculture	1·4	−1·1	−0·1	2·5	2·1
Manufacturing	3·2	1·4	0·9	1·8	1·9
Construction	4·6	3·5	1·7	1·1	1·3
Distribution	1·7	2·3	1·3	−0·6	−0·2
1937–51					
Agriculture	1·7	0·4	0·8	1·3	1·2
Manufacturing	2·5	1·0	2·9	1·5	0·9
Construction	−1·2	1·1	2·4	−2·3	−2·5
Distribution	−0·2	−3·2	1·2	3·0	1·6
1951–64					
Agriculture	2·6	−2·4	1·5	5·0	3·5
Manufacturing	3·2	0·2	3·3	3·0	2·0
Construction	3·8	1·6	6·2	2·2	1·8
Distribution	3·0	0·3	3·7	2·7	1·7

Source: R. C. O. Matthews and C. H. Feinstein (as Table 2.4).

Table 2.6 repeats the calculation of Table 2.3 for some individual sectors of the economy. Between the Wars, manufacturing achieved a growth of labour productivity of 1·8 per cent with very little investment and had a rate of growth of total factor productivity very much above the average for the rest of the economy; post-war it achieved a faster rate of growth of labour productivity but required a high rate of investment to do so, with the net result that T.F.P. was very much the same as the average for the rest of the economy, and no more than it had been for manufacturing in the 1924–37 period. The better average for the economy as a whole is to be explained by improved performance for the non-manufacturing sectors: notably agriculture (already high 1924–37, now exceptionally high), gas, electricity, water, transport, and distribution.

3 Technical change

We turn now to sketch the principal technical changes that altered economic life, that is, methods of production, the range of goods available to consumers, the economic habits of households; and also to discuss how the distinctive features of twentieth-century technical progress affected the international position of the British economy.

Road Transport

The most important technical factor operating in the U.K. affecting the organization of the economic activity of both firms and households continued to be the widening use of the internal combustion engine in road transport — a continuation of a process originating almost half a century before and already well developed in 1939.

Table 3.1 Transport: Goods traffic and Vehicles of all kinds

| | Goods Traffic (thousand million miles) | | Ratio to G.D.P. | Vehicles (thousands) | | | |
	Road	Rail		Cars	Buses	Goods	Total
1938	8–10	16·3	app 85	1944	53	495	3084
1949	17·8	22·0	116	2131	74	844	4108
1959	28·1	17·7	100	4966	77	1326	8662
1972	51·4	14·2	100	12740	77	1660	16117

The population of goods vehicles, already ½ million in 1938, had already increased by 50 per cent in 1948 and had doubled again by 1972 to 1·65 million. Numbers are an imperfect measure: the relative number of small vehicles grew fastest, but, on the other hand, the size of larger vehicles increased. The net effect on output of these changes was a doubling of ton-miles between 1938 and 1948 and a further tripling over the next twenty-five years. Measurement of output in ton-miles emphasizes too much the quantitative load-carrying aspects and leaves out of account the other characteristics of road transport that in one way or another reduce the costs borne by its users. Transhipment between different modes of transport has high costs in time, risk of delay, damage or loss, as well as in actual labour. To use road transport for whole journeys may avoid the need for transhipment altogether; or, when this is uneconomic, enables it to be done in places within the firm's control and co-ordinated with its own technical processes. Road transport also has flexibility that allows changes in routes or loads to be made at short notice.

The most obvious effect of road transport was in reducing the cost of carriage, so that concentration of production in larger units to serve much larger areas became feasible — for example, in baking and brewing, and perhaps most noticeably in quarrying and in other materials for the construction industry, where ability to deliver to a continually varying schedule of destinations was of special value. But we should not ignore a more complex effect. Together with the car which gave managers greater mobility, and the telephone which allowed them to exercise control from a distance, it permitted the development of more organized interdependence between widely separated productive units. Many of the advantages which economists, following Alfred Marshall, have termed 'external economies' and used to explain the advantages to firms of concentrating in particular areas are related to quickness and flexibility of communication. There is an advantage to firms in being in close touch with suppliers of components and customers; an advantage too, to both sides, in being able to meet unexpected demand by sub-contracting of production to other businesses suffering from lack of demand. These considerations were especially applicable to the twentieth-century engineering industry: the assembly of components lends itself to sub-contracting of production; and continual changes in the relative demand for different kinds of products, as well as in their design, required continual adjustment of sources of supply of components. The effect of road transport in the twentieth century was to increase the size of the areas within which external economies could be reaped: areas defined by an easy day's return journey.

Road transport made available in Britain the previously latent advantages of the compactness of the economy. And it may be that the industrial prosperity of the Midlands largely depended on the nearness to each other of what had hitherto been distinct centres of production. Why did this process take half a century to work out? Transport is to quite an extent concerned with transactions between businesses. Obtaining the advantages of motor transport therefore required adaptation of habits by both despatching and receiving firms. Indeed obtaining the full advantages often required the reconstruction, and even relocation, of plant. Such a process required a long time to complete and had barely begun between the Wars. Also the fall in road transport costs occurred gradually over a long period. In part this reflected the economies of vehicle production, where increasingly efficient design and the obtaining of economies of scale in production continued to reduce the relative cost of vehicles, at least until the 1960s. The reduction of operating costs was also delayed because the very growth of road transport led to congestion of roads. For more than ten years after the War there was a deliberate deferring of public investment in new roads; and it was only gradually, from the early sixties, that road improvements began to have an effect.

To some relatively small extent, the pace of growth of road transport was determined by the course of the decline of the railways. It was not until the 1960s that the closure of railways and the ending of their obligation to accept all traffic offered to them actually diverted much traffic to the roads through the non-availability of rail services. The proper social balance between rail and road transport was a matter of continuous battle for a good deal of the century between powerful vested interests (reinforced on the rail side by sentimental affection for an institution important in British history). It would be wrong, however, to see the growth of road transport solely as a result of victory in that battle. Much of the growth was not obtained at the expense of the railways. Furthermore, two independent factors operated in the post-war years to reduce the real advantages of the railways. The output of coal, in the transport of which they had a large comparative advantage and for which they had in many cases been built, was reduced; and some further reduction in the need to transport coal followed the development of the electricity grid as a means of transporting energy. The railways also had difficulty in adapting to the increasing level of real wages, in part because many of the technical improvements that were in fact invested in required very heavy investment and were only really advantageous if the volume of traffic increased; and in part because of the reluctance of a labour-force to accept changes in working practices which had grown complex and rigid in a century of monopoly.

Table 3.2 Passenger traffic (thousand million passenger miles)

	Bus	Car	Rail	Air	Total	Miles per head of population
1954	50·0	47·2	24·2	0·2	121·6	2395
1972	34·2	222·2	21·1	1·3	278·8	4997

Passenger Transport

In 1938 the number of cars registered was almost 2 million; severe wartime rationing of petrol reduced this number, and it was not reached again until 1948; during the following 25 years the number of cars increased 6½ times.

In this case the primary force operating was the rise in the incomes of families, together with, at least until the mid-sixties, a fall in the relative price of cars, reflecting the obtaining of economies of scale in production. The distinctive feature of car ownership is that once a family has committed itself to the substantial fixed costs of owning, licensing, and insuring, it is faced by only the marginal costs of running and will therefore use the car as much as it conveniently can. The consequence was often a near cessation of the use of public transport by some families. Despite a near-trebling of passenger movement from about 1950 (for work, leisure, and shopping) there was a levelling off of the growth of rail passenger transport and a considerable decline in public road passenger transport — abruptly reversing the rapid growth of the previous half-century. The decline in usage required operators either to provide less frequent services (or abandon them altogether) or to increase fares (which rising labour costs would already have required) — factors which may in turn have encouraged the rise in car ownership.

The growth of private car ownership increased the catchment areas from which businesses could draw their labour-force. Similarly, it had profound effects on the retail trade: it reduced the relative advantage of providing shops in the consumer's neighbourhood and of delivery to him; it increased the advantage of locations which offered the consumer either cheaper supplies because shops became large or self-service and self-delivery, or, in conjunction with other shops in a centre, gave a much wider range of choice.

Electricity

The second important change in the twentieth-century industrial revolution was the large scale production of electricity. During the period 1938–73 there was an eleven-fold increase in its consumption. Much of the increase in consumption came from the wider use of electricity to power machinery: already common in factories in the 1920s and in households in the 1930s. The advantages of such use of electricity were so large that their extension depended more on the achievement of economies of mass-production of electrically-powered equipment (including striking reductions in the cost of electric motors) than on further economies in the production of electricity. But they were reinforced by the geographical extension and standardization of the electricity supply that followed the nationalization of electricity in 1947.

In fact considerable economies in electricity production were achieved in the 1950s: through the introduction of equipment of increased scale which was both more economical in its use of coal (thermal efficiency increased from less than 20 per cent to over 30 per cent) and cheaper (the cost per unit of capacity in 1961 was only half what it had been in 1949); and through the continued development of the National Grid, which enabled fuller and more efficient use to be made of capacity. Whether the larger and cheaper supply of electricity triggered further significant development is doubtful. Most of the increased output was used to increase the temperature of homes and workplaces: a use which engineers frowned on because of its low efficiency as a use of energy; and which economists deplored because it required the building of many power stations that were not used most of the time because of the great variation of heating demand within the day and during the year. Some other industrial uses of electricity in the production of steel, chemical electrolysis, and the smelting of aluminium, were extended. But these applications were limited, and, in the case of aluminium, required large subsidies.

Further cost reductions were sought by two routes: the introduction of even larger scale generators and the harnessing of atomic energy. Both lines of development ran into technical problems of unanticipated difficulty and neither achieved its objective of reducing costs.

Materials

From the end of the nineteenth century the study of chemistry resulted in a more precise knowledge of the properties of materials, and systematic search led to the discovery of many new materials with distinctive properties. The obtaining of these materials on a commercial scale was greatly extended by the academic clarification of the general physical principles underlying chemical reactions, which, together with accumulation of the lessons of pioneering commercial development, provided the basis for the distinct technology of chemical engineering. Much of this development had occurred before the War (pioneered particularly by I. G. Farben in Germany) and some key products like nylon and polythene had been discovered in the U.S.A. and Britain. But it was the post-war period that saw the production of new materials on a large scale by continuous flow processes. These included the plastics, like nylon, terylene, polythene, polypropylene — some of which were attractive simply because of their cheapness, some because of superior qualities in their final use, and some because they were more easily used in manufacturing.

It is not clear how crucially dependent was the development of the chemical industry on the increasing use of petrol and relative cheapening of oil during the post-war period. The refining of petroleum for petrol led naturally to the search for uses of its by-products. Some new materials are technically more easily derived from petroleum than from other organic substances; and in some cases this advantage was reinforced by price. (At one stage in the 1960s the by-product naphtha was so cheap that it was said that coal would need to have been available free to compete with it.) No doubt this fact caused some products to be cheaper than they would otherwise have been; but whether such substitutions based primarily on small price difference (say of plastic for paper bags) were of critical importance is doubtful. Quite clearly many other developments within the chemical industry were quite independent: the accumulation of knowledge of how to produce various new substances whose qualities made them valuable products — for example, glues for industry, pesticides for agriculture, and, above all, pharmaceuticals.

To these developments, which we naturally think of as being the province of the chemical industry, we should add others, particularly the extension of the knowledge of the properties of metals and their alloys, but also of glass, ceramics, etc.

All these fields, where industrial research is a distinct activity not totally different in kind from the research of 'academic' laboratories, were areas in which British firms, from I.C.I. downwards, made important discoveries which they worked and licensed to others. Among developed nations the contribution of the U.K. in the post-war period was probably relatively high — a position manifested in a small surplus of licensing receipts over payments. In some cases, particularly steel alloys and other materials for use in aircraft, this performance was related to the sustained momentum of public expenditure on defence research.

Electronics

Radio production was well established before 1939. Television production had been pioneered before the War but had to wait until the 1950s to become a mass production industry. While the most profound effects of the innovation of television lie in the social and political fields, it was of economic importance not only in the employment directly given but also in its displacement of a service industry, the cinema, and its effect on the earning capacity of its 'stars'.

In the post-war period the electronic industry found a growing demand for other, more expensive, devices based on the valve and the cathode-ray tube — one area in which British industry had gained a wartime lead was radar. An important development was the invention of transistors as cheaper and robust substitutes for the fragile valve in 1947. But the industry continued to illustrate the paradox that advanced products may be primitively produced: the assembly of parts of television sets was occasionally 'put out' to housewives in their homes in the 1950s; and even though there was considerable rationalization of production through the use of printed circuits, the soldering iron remained an important tool only gradually displaced by the development of micro-circuits in the seventies.

Amongst other consequences, the transistor made more feasible the development of electronic computers for which some commercial applications were being found from the 1950s. But it was not until the middle or late sixties that the ability of these devices to automate clerical processes, and thereby assist in the processing of information for the control of organizations, and to control manufacturing processes directly, began to have profound effects on most parts of the economy. Early computers and uses for them had been developed in the United Kingdom. But despite this British companies failed, like those of other countries, to match the surging competition of I.B.M. and other American computer suppliers in the 1960s.

The telephone must also be mentioned. For most of the period the main change was an extension of the network from 1 ·5 million subscribers in 1935 to 12 ·7 million in 1975 and the completion of the change to automatic dialling. The second strand of development was of improvements to increase the carrying capacity of lines. The effect was to allow a considerable reduction in the real cost of all calls, the reductions being greater for trunk calls and greatest for international calls. This produced a tenfold increase in trunk calls between 1950 and 1975, and a seventy fold increase in international calls. Some of the increase was at the expense of letter traffic, which reached a peak in 1968. The postal services were faced with rising labour costs and little scope for labour-saving mechanization and were pushed into a vicious circle of increasing postal charges and reducing the quality of service.

Aircraft

British rearmament strategy in the 1930s, which was continued during the War itself, had given priority to aircraft production; and in the post-war period Britain remained the leading aircraft producer apart from the United States.

Until the War, aircraft were of no commercial significance in the U.K. except as objects of war production. American developments in body construction in the 1930s and the expansion of British productive capacity in the War subsequently made possible a considerable increase in commercial traffic. But it was in the 1950s that international travel was transformed by the application of a wartime development, the jet engine, which on the one hand reduced time taken in journeys and improved the comfort of passengers, and on the other hand allowed operators to increase the size and range of aircraft. The large scale of aircraft (and the focusing of demand on relatively few models) cut the capital costs of a unit of capacity somewhat, and vastly increased the productivity of the employees both of aircraft companies and airports, reducing prices to an extent that displaced ships as a means of passenger transport and built up transport of freight.

General features of technical change

The process sketched above was not solely or even mainly dependent on spectacular recent 'technological breakthroughs'. It was a continuation of changes already widespread before 1939 — the fundamental technical principles of which had been well established before the end of the nineteenth century, for example, in the cases of the internal combustion engine, electricity generation, and the telephone. Nor were ancient origins confined to fundamental principles: the automatic dialling systems being installed in the 1960s were a device invented by a Kansas City undertaker, Strowger, in 1889. There were some important apparent exceptions where development was rather quicker. A cluster of new plastic substances discovered in the 1930s became important industrial materials in the 1950s. Similarly, medical discoveries in the 1930s opened up a virtually new industry manufacturing drugs for chemotherapy. Again the invention of the transistor in

1947 made feasible digital computers that were already widely used within fifteen years. But even in this case the maximum effect of the innovation would take very much longer to emerge. And the economic benefits of other fundamental discoveries, notably atomic power, were not quickly tapped even though extensive resources were applied and significant technological developments were made. Atomic power had made little if any contribution before the end of the period to providing electricity generated at lower resource cost than coal-burning, though this stark fact was concealed by accountancy and inflation.

The most obvious reason why technical changes originating in one period may continue to increase the productiveness of an economy for half a century or more is the need for a great deal of more detailed technological advance to supplement and improve the original discoveries. This itself can be viewed as part of a process in which experience reveals to producer and consumer new possibilities for improvement and new applications. Though this involves many imaginative leaps, it can be regarded, in perspective, as an approximately continuous process occurring along a path opened up by the earlier more profound technological changes. Adaptation of design to the needs of users extends the market and brings economies of scale of production to supplement design economies, permitting price reductions and a further extension of the market. Extreme cases where economies of scale were very important were radio or television broadcasting, where a larger audience involved very little extra cost and permitted a vast increase in the quality of services provided at a given price. More usual examples, where cheapening was a consequence of increased scale of manufacturing production, were in cars, electric motors, television sets, plastics.

Two sources of economy of scale are distinguished by economists. One is economy of size of process. Within limits, the larger a chemical 'cooking pot' or an electrical generator the less it costs per unit of capacity to construct, and it can be run with less staff. The most noticeable cases, because they involve visibly large plant and considerable investments of capital, often fall almost entirely into this category. In the oil, chemical, pig-iron making, brewing, and shipping industries, much technical advance simply took the form of larger-scale plant that could be run by the same number of operators (or fewer if computerized controls were simultaneously introduced). But the source of much of the productivity increase of the period was the second kind of economy of scale and came from a greater specialization of function. In some cases, for example, the clothing industry, the specialization was primarily of labour concentrating on repetition of narrowly defined tasks: a source of economy not fundamentally different from Adam Smith's pin factory. In other cases, the reduction in costs might come from the dedication and adaptation of machines to the output of particular components. Such specialization might involve the use of rather more expensive machines for particular jobs, or simply the more intensive use of standardized machines.

Table 3.3 Size of plant in terms of employment (establishments with more than ten employees in manufacturing)

Number Employed in Plant	Percentage Total Employment			
	1935	1951	1963	1973
11–99	25·6	21·9	17·3	15·6
100–499	39·0	33·8	31·7	26·4
500–999	13·9	13·6	14·6	14·4
1000–1499	6·3	7·2	8·2	7·3
1500 and over	15·2	23·6	28·2	36·3

Source: K. D. George: *Industrial Organization* and 1973 Census of Production

Table 3.3 shows that during the period 1935–73 factories were increasing in size. Indeed, since the measure of size used is employment, the table may understate the increase in size because of the greater mechanization (and higher labour productivity) of larger factories. There are industries, for example chemicals and steel, where there are substantial economies to be made in carrying out related processes on the same site; and there was progress in exploiting these. But the technical advantages of such vertical integration are only important in rather special cases. What is more often important, particularly in industries involving engineering assembly, is proximity to a wide range of suppliers specializing in the handling of particular materials or particular techniques — in turn often relying on the existence of a working population with a wide range of skills. Such 'external' economies of industrial agglomeration seem, if anything, to have increased in the twentieth century with the greater production of complex products.

As described above, the increasing importance of particular goods is a partially self-sustaining process; falling prices obtain a wider market that increases scale of production and reduces costs, enabling prices to be further reduced. In mid twentieth-century Britain this process was powerfully boosted by two factors: by the road transport revolution, which permitted the concentration of production, and by the concurrent redistribution of income. The beneficiaries of redistribution were the class that had a disposition to spend a large proportion of their extra income on the products of manufacturing industry rather than, for example, services.

A further independent element was the increased demand for capital goods. Sometimes such an increase is attributed to the effect of rising real wages on labour costs. This cannot be the explanation, for in itself an increase in wages increases the price of capital goods too (since they embody labour). There will only be a substitution of capital for labour to the extent that the managers of capital accept lower rates of return. However, the fact that all businesses were subject to pressures simultaneously produced increases in the scale of demand for certain types of capital goods so that the costs of mechanization were lower and there was a wider range of experience generating 'learning economies' than there would otherwise have been.

The process of 'technological follow-through' as described above may seem to be an automatic generation of increasing benefits, but it contains certain tensions that provided many of the distinctive problems of the period for the managers of manufacturing business. As families become better-off they might want non-standardized products; and producers, as customers, might require capital goods adapted to the special requirements of their own production lines. Consequently, manufacturers needed to find a balance between standardization and variety. Perhaps even more acute was the further problem of reconciling the obtaining of economies of scale in the production of a product at a particular time with the adaptation of the product to incorporate the benefits of experience, especially if that adaptation involved a reorganization of methods of production, the tasks of members of the workforce, or the responsibilities of members of management.

Technology and Britain's international position

Britain in the third quarter of the twentieth century increased her commitment of resources to manufacturing. There are four possible types of explanation for the location of manufacturing in particular countries. The first, availability of natural resources, had been of importance to the U.K. in the nineteenth century, but, with the decline in the relative importance of coal and the opening up of richer resources of minerals elsewhere, no longer helped to explain the continuation in the mid-twentieth century of Britain's advantages as a site for manufacture. The second, production of goods which derive their value from the place of production, may have been of some importance for individual industries, for example Scottish whisky, but seems of little importance overall except in so far as the British location of production was accepted by customers as a guarantee of quality — and therefore conceals the operation of a different type of factor, that is, labour skill and reliability. The third explanation is innovation and consequent novelty of product. The final explanation is simply the advantages of long-established centres of industry based on economies of scale and agglomeration. These last two explanations require more detailed discussion.

Inventiveness, in the sense of the pioneering of novel devices, does not seem to have been of decisive importance in determining comparative industrial strength. There was no lack of inventiveness in the U.K., for example, in pioneering computing, or later, office calculators; but it is notorious that many British inventions were successfully commercialized elsewhere. Fundamental ideas moved easily from one country to another: sometimes they could simply be copied; in other cases, where the pioneer's position was protected by patents, a payment of royalties could obtain ideas worth much more than their cost.

At subsequent stages of development some technologies may be less mobile. They come to comprise vast collections of complementary pieces of knowledge about detailed techniques of production, methods of maintaining quality as well as basic principles. At any moment the pieces are distributed amongst individual employees of a firm or firms like pieces of a jigsaw, each one of which is of little use without most of the rest. 'Know-how' of this sort, together with access to an enormous range of complementary skills in the manual labour-force, underlay the U.K.'s position as a producer of jet engines and many other capital goods — though it should be observed that such supremacy was not obtained without continual costs of investment in development. Even this sort of 'know-how' is not completely immobile, because it may be to the interests of its pioneers to export it. This is particularly true where the production of capital goods is a specialized trade. Britain remained a more important producer of textile machinery than of textiles; or to take a more important case, was an exporter of plant for the iron and steel and the chemical trades.

But, it must be emphasized, the United Kingdom was an importer as well as an exporter of technology. This is illustrated (though not proved) by the fact that the flow of licence fees from the country was almost as large as the inflow. In particular there was an inflow of technology from the United States. This was a continuation of a process that had begun in the nineteenth century and presumably reflected the suitability of the U.K. as a place of manufacture, a place where long experience had bred a skilled labour-force accustomed to the discipline required in industry and a place where complementary supplies were obtainable.

Established centres of production (be they countries or districts of countries) frequently maintain their position for generations, and sometimes for centuries. The first explanation of this persistence is the effect of scale economies: the fact that the firm or industry already has a market sufficiently large for it to be able to offer its output at lower prices even than producers in locations more favoured by cheap materials or labour. The second factor is the effect of 'external economies'. Even if producers in new locations are willing to make a single sufficiently large investment to put up large plants, they will frequently be handicapped by the absence of complementary businesses nearby. This in turn may reflect the lack of a range of complementary know-how and skill among the local population. A third factor is 'learning economies': existing centres are in a position to be the closest observers of their own experience and may therefore learn most from it — rendering obsolete their own previous practices by the time they can be copied elsewhere.

The continued dominance of industrial activity shared by the

United Kingdom with relatively few countries in the twentieth century must largely be explained in these terms; and, in particular, the special importance of those branches of industry we label engineering which involve the assembly of the products of a wide variety of individual processes and continual modification of design.

Economies of scale and external economies in this way constitute a barrier, tending to preserve the advantages of established locations of industry. But they are also a cause of instability in competition between centres; a centre that gains a technological advantage may well find that as it gains markets it obtains cost advantages from economies of scale; while another centre which reaches a point where it begins to lose markets may find itself pushed into a process of cumulative contraction. Moreover the process of 'learning' does not always operate to the advantage of existing centres; the lessons of experience may sometimes be more clearly seen, or at least more willingly accepted, at a distance.

The importance of economies of scale was recognized in some of the contemporary thinking about industrial policy and economic policy more generally. For example, Professor Kaldor of Cambridge was emphasizing the desirability of a further shift of resources into manufacturing in the 1960s. He also thought that a growth of demand that came from exports, if necessary stimulated by devaluation, would be more beneficial than a growth of internal demand, because it would be concentrated on manufactures where there was most scope for obtaining economies of scale. And concern with the dangers of cumulative contraction in the face of competition from European centres was at the heart of his opposition to membership of the E.E.C. in the 1970s. Very much the same concern with economies of scale constituted an important part of the theories of 'virtuous' and 'vicious' circles that are discussed below (page 155). The view that there was scope for obtaining economies of scale underlay both the widespread acceptance of the need for concentration of industrial production in fewer firms and factories and the specific remedies advocated in the cases of particular industries. As with so many economic views, its validity as a justification for specific forms of intervention did not necessarily coincide with its validity as a descriptive judgment by detached external observers. The judgement that economies of scale in manufacturing were an important source of productivity gain was one thing; the opinion that the government should intervene to accelerate the process was another.

One final point must be made — the limited view of the observer, be he historian or administrator. Retrospectively it may be possible to chart the mainstreams and the dead-ends of technological change; but these may not have been so apparent at the time. More important, even a correct technological appreciation is not itself sufficient. The more easily available information is to decide the technological question, the more likely it is either that the market has already been captured or that entry to it has made competition so fierce that it is more advantageous to purchase than produce.

4 Productivity

Having looked at the nature of the technical change that was involved in the growth in output per head, we turn now to consider why that growth was distinctly slower than it might have been — a fact that was demonstrated by the international comparison presented in Chapter 2. As we saw there, the rate of growth of output per head in the U.K. was lower than in other industrial countries and continued to be lower even when the *level* of productivity overseas far exceeded that of the U.K. Although the growth of manufacturing productivity was not below the average of other sectors in the U.K., the gap between the U.K. and other countries was greatest in manufacturing.

Investment and productivity in the United Kingdom

During the period, it was widely held that an inadequate amount of investment was the primary cause of the low level of *per capita* output in the U.K. compared with other developed countries. It is almost certain that for a higher rate of growth to have been sustained there would have had to have been a higher level of investment — but this is not the same as saying that inadequate investment, in the sense of an exceptional unwillingness to accumulate and take risks by British capitalists, was the sole or even an important cause of the low growth.

As we saw earlier, the proportion of G.D.P. invested, while low in the immediate post-war period, increased substantially until the early seventies. During the sixties the capital stock was increasing distinctly faster than output. At the same time (possibly from the late 1950s) the rate of return on capital invested was falling. The simplest interpretation of this is that the opportunities for increasing output by capital investment were being exploited more quickly than new opportunities were emerging, so that investors were being pushed into comparatively less worthwhile uses for capital — that is, there were diminishing returns to capital implying a limited scope for increasing output per head by increasing capital per head. The argument is based on a very simple view of the economic system and is, by itself, not conclusive, because it assumes that profitability, the return to the owners of capital, is a good indicator of the total social return to capital. It might, in fact, happen that other causes were operating to reduce profitability by diverting the extra product of the investment almost entirely to labour.

An empirical approach is to make international comparisons. A study of investment and growth rates in Europe, North America, and Japan shows very little relationship between the growth of productivity and investment rates.

Figure 4.1 Investment and productivity growth 1955–67

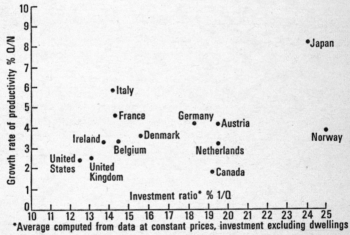

*Average computed from data at constant prices, investment excluding dwellings

Source: Organization for Economic Co-operation and Development (O.E.C.D.), *The Growth of Output 1960–1980.*

What such studies do reveal much more certainly is that the United Kingdom growth and productivity rates were low in relation to the amount of investment done. This suggests that some of the causes of poor productivity growth in the United Kingdom expressed themselves in the form of low return on capital investment to the country as a whole as well as to the owners of capital.

How do we account for popular opinion to the contrary? We should note that many observers were not disinterested; it is natural for work-forces, and for that matter managers, to say how much higher their productivity could have been if only those responsible for financing them had endowed them more generously with equipment. Official propaganda also naïvely emphasized the importance of increased productivity in each individual employment and neglected to take account of the cost of the resources absorbed in constructing and maintaining capital equipment — equipment that often lost its value rapidly because of obsolescence.

The international comparisons are entirely in aggregative terms. They do not preclude the possibility that there was inadequate investment in particular sectors of the economy because investible resources were used elsewhere — that is, investible resources were inefficiently allocated. One example of this might be the strong preference of private financial institutions in the early seventies, in face of declining industrial profitability and concern with inflation, to invest in office and commercial building. (This is not intended to endorse the view that such investment is inherently unproductive — merely that at any one time it might be overdone.) Another might be the encouragement given by plentiful government finance to building power-stations, which had a very high capital/output ratio, to meet a demand for heating by electricity that was unduly stimulated in the 1940s and 1950s. There were also cases of official sponsoring or encouragement of projects that were large users of capital and which had low or even negative social returns, for example, Concorde in the fifties and sixties or the aluminium smelter projects in 1967. Indeed it can be argued that the general system of investment incentives (mostly provided by modification of company taxation) tended to give a bias in favour of capital-intensive equipment that had no rationale in terms of social productivity.

There are, however, two other types of explanation for inadequate investment and for inadequate returns on investment. The most obvious is the inefficient use of investment when installed, because of inefficiencies of management and labour — this is the subject of the next section. The other explanation is in terms of inefficiences of the investment process itself that caused investment to be more expensive or less productive than it might have been.

In the modern world an investment decision is likely to involve a choice between alternative techniques, alternative sites, alternative 'phasing' of schemes for sequential construction. Too few managers in the U.K., which in the earlier part of the twentieth century had increased industrial output with relatively little new investment, had adequate experience of the complexities of such choices — which was reflected in the very crude accounting techniques that were used. But the inadequacies of accounting arithmetic were only one symptom (and the one most easily remedied) of a more general problem of investment management. In the forties and fifties an important part of the problem was the pressure on managements to maintain and increase production in the short run, which made it difficult to step back for long enough to think through investment plans with cool detachment. Moreover, when profitability was very high as it was in those years, professional managers, in making their decisions about investment, might pay most attention to intra-firm politics and personal empire building. Subsequently the pressure of current demand eased, and the compelling incentive of maintaining profitability increased, but industry was left with a generation of managers who had been conditioned in another world.

It is, however, wrong to see all, or most, of the problems coming from within the firm. Investment is not a matter of going to a shop and buying an article off a shelf. Major investment involves placing orders for the assembly by a contractor of various buildings and equipment — an activity that involves uncertainties of cost, timing, and performance of the completed plant. Some of these uncertainties are inherent in advancing technology, but many are affected by the efficiency of the contractor. Much of the contracting industry was notoriously inefficient. Some part of this may have been attributable to an ageing labour-force and the difficulty of recruiting foremen and middle managers, who were particularly important in an industry where tasks were not simple repetitions. But a great deal must be attributed to a prolonged period of excess demand for the services of the industry. With other products excess demand resulted in orderly queues, but in contracting an attempt could be made to carry out orders simultaneously. The result was that not only did orders take longer to complete because individual contractors found that they could not get the labour or materials they needed, but also that labour productivity actually declined because particular types of skilled labour found themselves waiting on particular sites either for materials or for the tasks of other grades of labour to be completed. Such experience had more lasting effects; for labour which experienced such periods of relief came to expect that only a part of the nominal working day would actually be used.

So far as the customers and potential customers of the contracting industries were concerned, the effects of this inefficiency only partly took the form of high prices paid for buildings and capital goods, which seemed to have risen more rapidly than prices generally. The inefficiency also extended the time taken for construction, increasing the time taken for outlays to become productive and making it more difficult to increase production early enough to take advantage of market opportunities, and, where obsolescence was fairly rapid, making the probable useful life of the equipment shorter than it need have been. Almost as bad, the time of completion was also unpredictable. This made planning complicated; and, also during the period of construction, required a continual supply of managerial effort to chivvy the contractors.

In the early seventies large projects in the United Kingdom might take half as long again to complete as overseas, with the constructional labour often less than half as productive. The net result was that although real wages were very much higher in the U.S.A., real constructional costs were little if at all higher there.

Government fiscal policy included explicit investment incentives. The effectiveness of such incentives may have been diminished by variations from year to year in their size and form which made it impossible for business to count with confidence on receiving them. For most of the period, the main form of incentive was an allowance for some proportion of investment expenditure against the taxable profits of the firm — thus confining the benefits to firms earning adequate profits; but from 1966 to 1970 unconditional investment grants were partially substituted for these allowances. Both grants and allowances discriminated between types of investment, favouring machinery over buildings and, in the case of grants, favouring what the government defined as 'industry' as contrasted with other economic activity. They were also part of the system providing incentives for investment in the regions of high unemployment. Ostensible purpose should not be confused with effect. For some industries and firms which found location in 'depressed areas' to be of no disadvantage, the *whole* system of allowances was simply an incentive to invest. By international standards, especially when regional incentives are included, investment incentives in the U.K. were high. And indeed part of their rationale was an attraction of foreign investment to the U.K.

While the government was directly encouraging investment, other parts of its policies hindered and distorted it. The positive incentives of grants for investment, provision of factories, and subsidies to meet removal costs proved inadequate to persuade enough industry to move quickly enough to the depressed regions. Resort was had to heavy-handed persuasion (in the case of cars and steel in 1959) and more generally a use of the power to refuse Industrial Development Certificates in prosperous areas from the later 1950s onwards. The use of this negative, coercive power is difficult to justify. It may well be right that industrialists should have been asked to consider relocation, and that substantial positive incentives should have been offered to them. But having demonstrated that they had reasons for staying where they were, reasons they considered more valuable than the considerable incentives offered, it might be thought that they had made their case.

It was said that in most cases transport costs were not large. This was true of the simple costs of lifting and carrying. But the economies of integrated, or close, sites are primarily economies of easy co-ordination and economy of managerial effort — important for all firms and crucial for medium-sized businesses. Thus, to an unknown but possibly considerable extent, the controls frustrated profitable extensions on existing sites. Furthermore, although the control was intended to control the demand for labour in prosperous areas, it did in fact operate by controlling the building of extra floor area. Consequently it was a deterrent to the rebuilding of factories to increase the floor area per head — a type of reorganization that is often essential for increased productivity.

To these controls as part of regional policy must be added the effects of town and regional planning — much extended by the

Town and Country Planning Act of 1947. The general constraining effect they had on industry can be regarded as a manifestation of the fact that land in Britain was relatively scarce, that a good deal of it had been spoilt in the past by unrestrained development, and that industrialists could not expect to have the low costs of green-field sites without question. But the bureaucratic administration of these controls mingled with the operation of Regional Policy and the inefficiency of the contracting industry to increase the amount of managerial effort involved in invesment. It also probably increased costs, and certainly extended the interval between decisions being made and their resulting in increased output.

Labour productivity

While an important part of the relative unwillingness of British businesses to invest derived from the inefficiency of the process of investing, this was probably not as important a cause as the relative lack of productivity of the investment when in use in the U.K. The most vivid evidence is provided by observations, made at various times, that even when using comparable equipment, the productivity of labour in Britain was lower than elsewhere. L. Rostas, in his 1948 study *Comparative Productivity in British and American Industry*, noted that 'in a number of industries (or firms) where the equipment is very largely identical in the U.S. and U.K., e.g. boots and shoes, tobacco, strip-steel (or in firms producing both in the U.K. and U.S. in such fields as electrical appliances, soap, margarine, etc.) there are still substantial differences in output per worker in the U.K. and the U.S.' In the mid-sixties the Chemical E.D.C. (Economic Development Council) reckoned that a change in attitudes and practices could, on their own and without other change, produce a manpower saving in the industry of 20 per cent. The Central Policy Review Staff in their 1975 *Report on the British Car Industries* said 'It takes almost twice as many man hours to assemble similar cars using the same or comparable plant in Britain as it does on the Continent . . .'; and in a wider study of productivity differences between branches of the same company in the U.K. and overseas, C. F. Pratten in 1976 found smaller differences — but ones which were made more significant because they could not be attributed to variations in managerial ability.

The most obvious explanation of low labour productivity is the 'restrictive practices' of the labour force: unwillingness, because of boundaries between skilled trades, to accept a wide range of tasks; insistence on man-to-machine ratios that were excessive in relation to the technology; maintenance of conventional modifications to the workday — tea breaks on the one hand, excessive overtime for the purpose of generating extra earnings on the other. To which might be added a willingness to employ productivity-reducing sanctions, 'working-to-rule', to enforce the maintenance of the *status quo*.

Many restrictive practices were of long standing, originating in the pre-1914 U.K. economy where unemployment was persistent and where the skilled trades, although normally more continuously employed, had the memory of episodes of complete displacement through technological change. Restrictive practices had been accepted by employers because the scarcity and price of labour changed very slowly — as did the technology of processes. Other restraints by the labour-force on output per man were derived from memories of inter-war unemployment. In some cases, however, the motivation was related to the process of wage-bargaining: a rigid maintenance of the *status quo* so that employers did not introduce more economical practices without 'paying' for them. Other practices like tea breaks seem simply to have grown and come to be regarded as a perquisite.

Restrictive practices and other causes of low productivity were often not related to the policies of unions. They varied from firm to firm or plant to plant and were maintained by the informal organization of shop-stewards, or simply by the inertia of the labour-force. It was often said in the period that many restrictive practices were a consequence of inefficient management. This view was expressed in 1968 by the Donovan Commission on Trade Unions following the National Board for Prices and Incomes: 'the more important reason is the acceptance by management of low standards of performance as normal' and 'the main deficiencies would seem to be in organization and the use of modern labour management techniques.' Thus, for example, failure to keep a work-force steadily employed because of poor scheduling of work was likely to lead to a permanent decline in the amount of work that the work-force expected to do. It seems rather too simple to blame management for not being sufficiently tough in enforcing 'discipline' without paying attention to the general environment — particularly the high level of employment that existed for twenty-five years; and it is setting unrealistic standards to say that management should have been able to cope with any labour-force however intransigent. On the other hand, management in its dealings with labour was insufficiently far-sighted in the long period in the 1940s and 1950s when production in the short term was the pressing priority and settlements were made without regard to the long term precedents they set. It was also the case throughout the period that the growing size of companies and their extensive reorganization led to a diversion of management talent from the management of men.

The restrictive practices and attitudes of a labour-force often directly hindered investment — especially where it involved the introduction of new techniques. The labour-force may have had justifiable fears of redundancy — or it may have seen the introduction as an opportunity for the extraction of a 'toll' in increased earnings. From the management's point of view there were two types of problem: first, the revision of working practices needed to justify the investment required complex, and, where several unions were involved, multilateral negotiations. Second, with investment involving radical innovation there could be a great deal of uncertainty about exactly what new working practices would be required. Managers were faced with the dilemma of either making extensive commitments in advance sufficient to overcome the opposition of the most stubborn union, or going ahead with the investment and bargaining after the investment had been made. The latter was a dangerous policy for it made it possible for a union to extract the whole extra output as increased earnings, leaving virtually no return to the capital sunk in the investment. Unions generally might act with restraint perceiving their long term interest in encouraging investment, but there were cases where managements found themselves in a very weak position. (Similarly there were notorious cases in the 1970s where constructional workers extracted large bonuses by threatening to strike as oil-rigs neared completion.)

The existence of restrictive practices in a labour-force is not always an impediment to innovatory investment. Indeed, there are examples, as in wool-combing in the mid-nineteenth century, where it was a powerful incentive. Such direct displacement of restrictive labour was virtually impossible in mid-twentieth-century Britain, because of the strength of the sanctions that were accepted as legitimate for a labour-force to employ. But less direct substitution did occur: part of the economy of roll-on, roll-off sea carriage of road transport was due to avoiding the inefficiency of dockers' handling; and, indeed, more generally, part of the economy of road transport was that it reduced the amount of transhipment, a function notorious for inefficient labour throughout the ages; or, to take a different example, some part of the growth of office machinery may have been a consequence of the restrictive practices of labour in the printing trades.

It would be wrong to blame all the inefficiency of British industry on the restrictive stubborness of its manual labour-force. During the fifties and sixties the U.K. attracted many foreign companies, particularly from the U.S.A. The U.K. branches of these companies generally had higher manual productivity, and higher profitability than the average of British industries: and, indeed, higher profitability than U.K. based companies working overseas. Their superiority was not always related to the exploitation of new products, though it was often a consequence of good marketing management in the broadest sense — that is, devising (and subsequently revising) a range of products that is attractive to customers yet at the same time is compatible with productive efficiency. Prima facie there is therefore a case for emphasizing managerial inefficiency. (However, it should be remembered that incoming firms do have an advantage in being able to choose their location and, particularly, in setting the terms on which they engage their labour-force, whereas the managements of established firms have to cope with a situation they have inherited.)

It needs to be noticed that examples of low labour productivity are easiest to identify where direct comparisons are possible and the output is measurable — which is most usual in manual occupations. However, if inefficient employment had been confined to manual labour, the ratio of 'white collar' to 'blue collar' labour in the U.K. would have been especially low. But it was not.

An increase in the average level of labour productivity in an economy can be thought of as the outcome of two processes: the increase of labour productivity in specific occupations; and the movement of labour from less to more productive occupations. The discussion so far has been entirely about the first of these. W. E. G. Salter in *Productivity and Technical Change* (Cambridge, 1966) estimated that between 1924 and 1950, that is, including not only the inter-war period but also the wartime period when there was such large growth in the size of manufacturing industry, shifts in the distribution of labour accounted for about half of the increase in average productivity. R. Wragg and J. Robertson in a comparable study for the period 1954–73 *Post-war trends in employment* (D. of E., 1978) estimated that less than a tenth of the increase in productivity was due to a change in the distribution of labour between industries.

There was a difference between Britain and Europe in this respect; in Europe the industrial work-force could grow by migration from peasant agriculture (and also, in the case of West Germany, by immigration of East German refugees). It may be, moreover, that the net gain from such labour mobility was more than a matter of the arithmetical difference in average productivities. A flow of labour from the countryside tends to be of an exceptionally mobile and malleable type; being young, willing to move to the places where it is most needed, and having no preconceptions about the way in which it should work.

This contrasts strongly with the supply of labour that is the product of industrial redundancy, older, often unwilling to move, and less willing to adapt.

Explanations of several kinds can be found for the relatively low movement of labour in the U.K. The increased average age of the labour-force and the high proportion of married women were demographic factors which naturally produced lower mobility. The housing shortage and housing policy gave established tenure of a rented property value that was lost by movement; while the system of local queues in the allocation of council houses gave an incentive to stay put. Again there was some shift of public attitudes: the Barlow Report (1940) endorsed the view that workers had a right to expect work to be brought to them; while the administration of unemployment relief post-war imposed rather less pressure to search for and take whatever jobs were available than it had before the War.

Some general factors affecting labour productivity

Table 4.1 Percentage age composition of economically active population

		1901	1931	1951	1966
Male:	under 20	12·9	10·7	5·6	5·9
	20–24	10·0	7·0	6·7	6·4
	25–44	30·0	29·0	31·0	25·7
	45–64	15·0	20·3	22·9	24·0
	over 65	2·8	3·2	3·0	2·3
Females:	under 25	15·5	14·0	10·3	9·7
	25–44	9·1	10·3	11·8	12·3
	45–64	3·7	4·7	8·0	12·6
	over 65	·8	·7	·7	1·1

The decline in population growth from its nineteenth-century rates affected the age composition of the labour-force as well as the age composition of the population. In 1901, only 25 per cent of the male working population were over 45, but by 1966, 40 per cent were. In manual occupations, like mining or construction, this produced a relative imbalance in the labour-force — a lack of physically fit young men to do the heavy work. More generally, it may have produced an unwillingness to introduce change; a resistance to change by skilled labourers who felt themselves unable to adapt. Similar effects were likely to occur at every level of the hierarchies of industrial management.

The increased numbers of female employees mitigated some shortages, supplying many very relevant qualities and skills, particularly in lighter industry, administration, and the service trades. But there was some limitation of the range of types of occupation which women were able or willing to fill, given that many were married and an increasing proportion over 45.

It was fashionable in the sixties to argue that expenditure on education, as well as the replacement of part of the working life by a longer period of education, should be regarded as a productive investment in 'human capital'. It is certain that many employments in the 1970s did require higher levels of education than had been needed in 1937. But it is not apparent either that the educational programmes introduced were, in most cases, designed primarily to improve efficiency in subsequent employment, or that they were particularly effective in doing so. That employers increased their formal educational requirements seems to be a consequence of regarding successful survival of the education and examining process as an indicator of basic ability as much as of proficiency in peculiarly relevant skills. It is, moreover, arguable that changes in access to higher education, particularly after the Education Act of 1944, but also as a consequence of improving real incomes throughout the century, sieved talent and diverted it away from manufacturing occupations in which it would previously have come to rest.

Government industrial policy

Throughout the period governments proclaimed their concern with industrial efficiency. They intervened in the working of the economy by general fiscal incentives, by financing research and development, by assisting the finance of specific projects, by holding enquiries into the problems of specific industries (cotton and wool textiles, shipbuilding, the car industry) and providing finance to carry out the recommendations of these enquiries, by setting up in 1961 the National Economic Development Council as a forum for discussion of the problems of industry, and by general proclamation of the benefits of increasing productivity. However, much of the intervention was undertaken in pursuance of other more immediate, or more narrowly defined, objectives.

The fact that the country was almost continuously in balance-of-payments difficulties caused the govenment to consider policies on the grounds that they would 'save imports' or 'earn foreign currency'. Outstanding examples of such policies were agricultural policy, the purchasing of items like computers or aircraft, the aluminium smelter projects of 1967, the hotel grants scheme of 1968 to promote tourism, and the provision of export credit. The difficulty with such policies, even in terms of their own objective, was that while the most visible direct balance-of-payments benefits and costs could be measured, the indirect consequences could not. This was a result of imperfections of information: encouraging home meat production visibly saved meat imports, but exactly how much did it lead to increased imports of feeding stuffs? There was also a divergence between the short and long term advantages of such actions: the cost of 'saving imports' was the use of resources that could have been shifted to other users in the long run. If the exchange rate had been used to reflect the scarcity of foreign exchange and had been reflected in the relative prices, and therefore in the relative profitability of exporting and of competing with imports, resources would have moved naturally to save foreign exchange and might have done so more efficiently — as indicated by greater profitability or absence of need for subsidy. Government policies adopted may have been justified by urgency: if balance-of-payments problems were immediate, their remedy could not await the working out of 'natural processes'. But the degree of naïvety in the mercantilism practised by government was also determined by limitations to the subtlety of arguments it could present to the general public and indeed to many professional politicians.

Government policy towards research and development might have been expected to be closely related to long term economic efficiency. In fact international comparisons show that although in the 1950s and 1960s the U.K.'s expenditure on research and development was, relative to national income, high, its allocation seems to have had little relationship to economic efficiency.

In themselves, scientific and technical progress do not constitute economic progress. They are intellectual achievements of which a country may be proud; but in economic terms they are absorbers of resources, sometimes in considerable quantity. They are transmuted into economic progress by the introduction of new commercial products and the replacement or improvement of existing methods of production. Often the second is merely the obverse of the first; a new product is itself often a machine or material to be adopted by other firms. Innovation in its early stage requires from managers not only vision of possible uses, but perception of consequences, and it may require considerable diplomatic effort in dealing with customers and work-force. An important element both in product innovation and improvement of production technique may be the imitation of others' experience, which may involve payments for patented products or know-how, or simple observation.

Distortions of the innovatory process, from an economic point of view, can occur because too many resources are devoted to obtaining technical progress in particular sectors; because too much effort is devoted to innovation of products, and too little to a more widespread exploitation of them; or because there is too much concern to be original and distinctive. The latter is a fundamental problem because the activity of research and development is likely to involve the harnessing of the creativity of scientists and technologists. The difficulty is compounded where there are decisions to be taken by politicians who are concerned to be seen to be patriotic and to be the godfathers of attractive projects. A further difficulty that arises with politicians, civil servants, and in the bureaucracies of private firms is the vested interests of individuals in not being seen to have been wrong — a concern inconsistent with matters in which there may be considerable uncertainty and a need to try a succession of different lines of approach.

The War had begun with the success of radar, and ended with the atomic bomb. Its legacies were: the existence of sizeable groups with vested interests in particular areas of technology, especially aircraft; a particular view of the nature and role of R. & D. among government and civil servants; and a degree of credulity among most of the population. But there were considerable dangers in applying to peacetime a view of technical progress that was appropriate to military matters: the premiums to be attached to absolute superiority in technical performance (for example, extra speed in aircraft) were likely to be much less in civil life; similarly the premium for being first and the disadvantages of copying were less; the disadvantages of relying on overseas purchase were very much less; and with weapons a greater part of innovative effort went into the weapon and less into its subsequent employment than was the case in many areas of peacetime economic activity.

All three legacies detracted from the effectiveness of R. & D. in the U.K. Quite disproportionate amounts of R. & D. resources were devoted to items like aircraft and atomic energy. In looking at R. & D. there was too much attraction to the novel and spectacular, there was also too much concern with *domestic* innovations — a preference that might be justified by mercantilist arguments but which often degenerated into simple nationalistic sentiment not significantly different from the loyal support of local sports teams. Related to this was too much concern for the interests of the producers of the innovating products, and too little for their customers, coerced into accepting reduced productivity from equipment imperfectly suited to their needs. Last, but by no means least, talk by politicians and press of 'the white heat of technology' reinforced an impression left by the War and cultivated in the public mind a picture of technological progress by the production of fundamental inventions that would eventually bring forth large benefits quite apart from the everyday activities of everyone as a producer. (Rather in the way that the same war left some South Sea islanders demoralized by 'cargo cults').

A distinct cause of intervention was 'job-preservation'. Firms or industries in difficulty, or the representatives of their labour-forces, sought subsidies or other favourable intervention in order to avoid factories closing down. Such pleas became more frequent as the general level of unemployment increased in the later sixties. Quite often, as the cases were presented, industrial efficiency seemed also to be at stake. Sometimes investigating committees made plausible cases for government assistance to improve the industries' performance, as with Cotton (Steel 1969) or Shipbuilding (Geddes 1966) or Cars (Ryder 1975). It would be naive to see such enquiries as detached assessments. However objective the committee members were ,they started from the political fact that their own appointment was an acceptance of a prima facie case for intervention; and their view was limited to the industry itself and not to alternative uses of its resources. In general they tended to make the most optimistic assumptions they could instead of passing dispassionate judgement on the basis of previous performance.

Such comments may seem to imply the existence of some alternative, more far-sighted and dispassionate, strategy that might have been adopted. This implication is not intended. On the contrary, not only is the course of technological change and its implications something that is not susceptible to any simple generalization, but also, and more important, in a competitive world deductions cannot easily be drawn from technological facts about the most appropriate economic policy. The production of novel devices may be an overcrowded market; as may be the exploitation of processes where there are economies of scale. Indeed the sort of engineering economies most visible to the external observer, while necessary to ensure competitiveness, are unlikely to be sufficient, for they will be the features that are most easily matched elsewhere. By the time the component causes of the commercial success of a product are recognizable (certainly by the time they can be agreed upon by a government committee) they are unlikely to provide a basis for specialization — except for imitation by an economy that accepts that its labour will be cheap.

In the absence of firm generally agreed technical or economic criteria for long term 'industrial strategy', industrial policy was dominated by the objectives of saving foreign exchange and saving jobs, which were interpreted crudely and short-sightedly. On these matters it is unclear whether contemporary advances in economics and the wider employment of economists made any useful contribution. Economic analysis provided a vocabulary and provided modules of logical argument. Unions and industrialists consequently learned to put forward their cases in plausible economic terms. But neither their advocacy nor government's response was founded on dispassionate pursuit of economic truth. Used in this limited way, economic logic became little more than a fashionable type of rhetoric. This is not to say that the whole outcome was determined by vested interests. In part the policy outcome was the consequence of the interests of both ministers and senior administrators in being seen to do something spectacular in the short run, and to be pursuing policies that seemed most obviously related to the objectives of avoiding unemployment, improving the balance-of-payments, and at the same time enhancing national pride. Policies came to be determined by their 'presentability' and governments became prisoners of their own propaganda.

Some general reflections

It is sometimes suggested that the poor post-war performance of the U.K. economy was related to not having been defeated in the War and not having had the opportunity of making a fresh start. It is difficult to see the force of this argument in material terms.

If British capital had been obsolescent in the immediate post-war period, it could have been replaced with new machinery at the same cost in resources as in other countries, apart from demolition costs. And while demolition costs in some cases are not completely negligible, it would be absurd to contend that they were of a size sufficient to outweigh the positive value of the rest of the productive machine that was inherited in 1945. For most British capital was not in fact obsolescent in the immediate post-war period; a lot of it was of quite recent construction. That it had some life left in it was, in material terms, an unqualified advantage.

If there is anything in the argument (or in the not dissimilar 'disadvantage of the early start') it must be expressed not in terms of machines but of people and organizations. Victory brought with it a relative lack of incentive to seek for, and accept changes in, techniques and methods of work that would be conducive to economic growth, and the war experience had bred inappropriate assumptions about the relative importance of different managerial tasks.

An aggregative, distant, economist's perspective of the process of technological change is valuable in taking us away from the particularities and discontinuities of the individual case, but is misleading if taken too literally. Technological change is not a process in which a growth-producing stimulant simultaneously and continuously operates with even effect on all parts of the economy — like a fine drizzle of fertilizer. In detail the process is not continuous but involves discrete steps, often sizeable steps, forward. Moreover, while the benefits of most innovations may be very widely diffused, they are not necessarily evenly diffused. Frequently benefits are scattered amongst consumers, while costs are concentrated on particular parts of the labour-force (including managerial labour) in the form of redundancy or lowered premium value of their special skills — either because their product has been superseded (galvanized buckets displaced by plastic buckets) or because improved machines have reduced the need of their special skills. Nevertheless, it could be argued that since producers are (in spending their incomes) consumers, everyone will derive a net benefit from technological change. However, even if this were the case, the fact that the process of technological change is divisible means that to individuals it may be quite rational to oppose, or at least impede, technical change in the field in which they are producers, while hoping to enjoy the benefits of progress elsewhere.

Unwillingness to accept change is likely to be diminished if it occurs in an industry for which demand is expanding rapidly, since this makes redundancy less likely; and it should also be less the lower the general level of unemployment. But even if unemployment is low, labour may be unwilling to contemplate movement voluntarily — particularly if it is middle-aged and fears or simply dislikes disturbance. How successfully workers can oppose change might seem to depend primarily on the strength of employers *vis-à-vis* workers. But this is to over-emphasize the opposition of the two classes. Except in the short run, or in special cases where technical change relieves employers of particularly wearing labour problems, the benefits of technical change are eventually likely to be passed on to customers. The most effective pressure on managers to innovate is their exposure to competition. An increase in the number of producers or potential producers makes it more likely that there will be some firms that do see advantage in the new process, and by their actions or their reputation they stir the other firms to counter-measures. Exposure to overseas competition is more likely to produce this effect, as is exposure to the competition of products that are substitutes economically but are produced by other industries. During the War, and in some areas for fifteen years afterwards, producers had a seller's market at home which was also insulated by high tariffs. The normal forces of competition were suspended and a generation of workers and managers grew up rather like a generation of farmers who had never experienced any variation of the climate.

It is indeed instructive to consider the case of British agriculture. It can be argued that the system of producer subsidies overstimulated home production, but, from the break in the seller's market in the early fifties until the entry into the E.E.C., the industry was exposed to changing conditions which threatened farmers' incomes. The industry adapted by mechanizing, consolidating holdings, and releasing labour. The industry itself cannot take complete credit for the very large gains in the productivity of labour and in Total Factor Productivity (see page 28) that occurred, but it provides a model of successful exploitation of the innovations provided for it.

Alternatively, we might consider retail distribution. Although many firms increased in size the sector became more, rather than less, competitive and, by contrast with the inter-war period, there was a willingness to compete for custom in price as well as service, with the result that there was an adaptation to the needs of customers and the sector was accepted as being one which did not lag behind other countries.

5   Business institutions

In 1975 about eighty per cent of G.D.P. was the output of institutions comprising 'the market economy', that is, businesses and individuals depending primarily on revenue from sales of their products or services to cover their costs (as contrasted with those branches of government and local government whose costs were met by administrative allocation of revenue from taxation). Fifty of the eighty per cent was the output of 'companies', eleven of 'public corporations', and nineteen of 'persons' (a somewhat misleadingly entitled category since it included some miscellaneous organizations like universities, but it mainly consisted of small unincorporated businesses and the self-employed).

The proportionate importance of 'the private sector', that is, companies and persons, had been reduced between 1938 and 1955 by the 1945 Labour Government's programme of nationalization, and it declined again from the mid-sixties because of the growth of government. However (making some allowance for the inclusion in the 'private sector' of miscellaneous organizations), in 1975 two-thirds of G.D.P. was produced and two-thirds of employment was provided by businesses in private ownership — principally by companies.

Despite extensive amendments to company law, the legal form of companies remained essentially unchanged: institutions to be run by their directors in the interests of their owners, the shareholders. In practice, however, there were fairly considerable changes brought about by the changing nature of ownership, changing technology, and by increasing needs for external finance — changes which took the form of the increasing size and organizational change of companies themselves, and of changing roles of financial institutions. This institutional evolution will be the first and main subject of this chapter.

Figure 5.1 Share of 100 largest firms in manufacturing net output

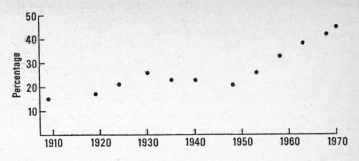

Source: L. Hannah: *The Corporate Economy* (Methuen, 1976).

Growth of firms

Figure 5.1 shows that the share of the 100 largest manufacturing firms in the net output of manufacturing increased from 15 per cent in 1909 to 23 per cent in 1939 to 45 per cent in 1970. There were similar trends in other parts of the economy: in retail distribution, in finance, and in the provision of many services. The chart shows a perceptible halt, possibly a reversal, of this trend during the period 1930–48 (with the share of the 100 largest firms falling from 23 per cent in 1935 to 21 per cent in 1950). Growth in the relative size of large firms in other periods took place to a very large extent by the process of absorption by amalgamation (of previously independent businesses); and there was a relatively low number of amalgamations between 1935 and 1948. Possible explanations of this were that the recovery of the thirties and the War brought higher profits and that, though these were heavily taxed, the financial position of firms was more secure than in the depressed 1920s. This, however, would explain only the slowing down, not the reversal, of the trend. One possible explanation would be that, apart from amalgamation, larger firms grew more slowly than smaller firms. However, examination of individual industries shows that there were about as many cases where large firms gained market share as those where they lost. This pushes us into emphasizing that in the period 1935 to 1948 there was a very marked change in the pattern of output because of the increased proportion of exports and capital goods, so that a larger proportion of manufacturing output was accounted for by sectors where the largest firms (of *that* time) were not so important.

From 1948 the proportionate importance of the largest firms in the whole economy resumed its growth, and almost doubled in twenty years. There are two fundamentally different types of explanation for this change: that it reflected the technical advantages of producing in larger units; and that it was a consequence of financial forces that would still have operated strongly even if there had been no economies of scale in the use of resources.

A significant fact is that there was much more growth in size of firm than in size of factory. In 1935 half of total employment was in factories with under 300 employees; in 1973 half was still in factories with under 700 employees, an increase in size 2⅓ times. When we look at firms instead of factories, in 1935 half employment was in firms with under 400 employees; whereas in 1973 half was in firms with under 4,500, a more than tenfold increase in size. It may have been the case in 1973 that firms had merged, but were still in the course of concentrating their production by building new plant and closing old plant, but this cannot explain very much of the contrast. The logic of most mergers was not to be explained in terms of factory size — particularly those mergers, of which there were many, between quite large firms often producing different products.

There were many important technical economies of scale of operation not dependent on the size of individual factories. For example, a food manufacturer found important economies in advertizing, processing orders for, and delivering, a range of products. In relation to this we may notice the growing importance of the economies of large-scale advertizing (on television and in the national press), and the scope for achieving fuller loading of delivery vehicles of ever increasing size. Other types of economy could be found in the field of management, and depended on the fact that a particular branch of a business required much more management effort at certain times; for example, when new products were to be introduced, or extensions to be made, a large firm could meet this need by shifting managers, and in some cases obtain extra advantages from their specialization in particular tasks.

This sort of argument emphasizes the advantages of merger to the managements which survive to reap the advantages of scale. It does not look at matters from the point of view of the businesses that were absorbed and their managers. In a simple world of theory, in which all advantages were visible and all individuals acted to maximize their profits, it would be possible to devise a bargain where any merger had net advantages. However, gains were not necessarily visible, the managers in control would not necessarily share fully in the compensation received by owners, and in any case owners might attach great value to independence itself. In practice mergers are as much products of the pressure of events as the pull of prospective benefits.

What kinds of pressure persuaded owners and managers to abandon their independence? Some of these pressures came from an increasingly hard environment. The average level of return on capital may have shown no decline in the 1950s, but the effort required and risks involved in achieving that profit had already begun to increase in industries where customers were no longer patiently waiting in queues and where the size of rivals was no longer restricted by wartime allocations of resources. The growth and improvement of road transport increasingly threatened the position of firms that had hitherto had local monopolies (for example, in brewing). In other markets competition was increased by the Restrictive Practices Act of 1956, which, as interpreted by judges, effectively prohibited the making of agreements between firms to avoid competition in price, to share business, and the like — practices that had been important in the lean markets of the inter-war period in many industries. Some of the increased competition was, of course, a consequence of the increasing scale of rival firms. But not all of this was a consequence of the benefits of scale on their costs. For increased size also brings increased bargaining power, which firms can use in their dealings with their customers and their suppliers, as well as in the threats of ruinous competition that they can make directly against rival firms.

Independent existence, particularly for small specialized businesses, was also involving increased risks. Total output may have been subject to very much less violent fluctuations than before 1939, but costs were also less variable because labour required to be given more continuous employment. It was a world where changing technology required more specialized capital equipment (with uncertainty about how rapidly it would become obsolete); and when competition took the form of the introduction of new products, considerable sums had to be sunk in developing the product and in launching it, with a risk of complete loss.

In the case of family businesses, heavy taxation had conflicting effects. (These were probably already manifest in the 1930s, when taxation was much higher than it had been at the beginning of the century, but were intensified by the increases of the Second World War.) High levels of corporate taxation directly reduced the finance available to business, but high levels of taxation on 'unearned' income made the alternative of living on dividends unattractive. And, so long as there were generous tax allowances for capital expenditure, it was still possible to accumulate fortunes within a business. Moreover, high levels of taxation of personal income made some aspects of a manager's activities that were allowable as business expenses relatively more attractive. With time the balance may have shifted: from 1957 it became less easy to accumulate funds in businesses; large family businesses were compelled to distribute and accept high levels of personal taxation on their profits; from 1964 there was the prospect that when a business was ultimately sold the capital gains would be taxed; and from 1974 the Capital Transfer Tax made the transfer of property much less easy than it had been under the previous system of Estate Duty.

The oldest explanation of the end of family businesses is 'failure of succession'. As late as the 1940s businesses were likely still to be looking for successors among large families born in Victorian times. But subsequently the successor had to be sought from generations where there had been smaller numbers of children (as well as smaller numbers of nephews). At the same time the wider availability of higher education may well have diverted children from wishing to take over family businesses.

The largest number of mergers were of the kind described above: owners, often families, deciding to sell the businesses they ran either because of the attractive offers they received or because of the adverse circumstances they encountered. However, the most important feature of the post-war period, 'the take-over bid', had its distinctive effects on firms in which the shareholding owners did not actively manage the business, or have any effective say in its running. By making a successful offer directly to shareholders, a bidder could displace an incumbent management against its will. The 1948 Companies Act contributed to the feasibility of bids by extending requirements for the publication by directors to shareholders of more accurate accounts. Without this, outside bidders would not have known where there were companies whose income or share price was low in relation to the assets controlled.

Bids to shareholders were first employed in the early 1950s by a few individuals (one of the best known being Sir Charles Clore) who were attracted by cash and easily marketable property, which in the case of some companies exceeded the current market value of the shares. Once control of the company was obtained, the assets were used to finance bids for further companies, which accumulated in conglomerate empires, sometimes known as industrial holding companies. It might have been expected that the opportunities for this type of operation would soon have been exhausted as firms themselves drew on their resources to finance investment in the 1950s and 1960s, and as share prices rose. However, the course of industrial change, together with the rise in property values, created new opportunities. Firms came to have branches or subsidiaries whose profitability was low in relation to the value of the assets employed — a value that could be realized by a bidder lacking any sentimental motives for keeping unprofitable branches in existence. In other cases the opportunity depended on the resale of businesses to other firms with which their operations could be combined. Throughout the 1960s, the conglomerate empires grew, and new ones like that of Mr. Jim Slater were born. Some were to wilt and die in the financial crisis of 1972–5 — usually through having borrowed too much on optimistic expectations about property and share values which their own growth had done so much to promote.

The late 1950s saw a further development. Bids were made by companies whose professional managers wished to acquire businesses which, in one way or another, they thought could be fitted into their existing firms, and for which they usually paid by exchanging shares in their own companies for those in the company taken-over. The first major engagement of this sort was the contest for British Aluminium in 1958; and one of the most notable, for being unsuccessful, was the attempt by I.C.I. to take over Courtaulds in 1961.

Our view should not be confined to visible conflicts. The increased difficulty of defending weak positions made managers much more willing to agree to merger proposals if they thought that their chances of successfully appealing to shareholders were small, or if they were interested in their prospects as managers in the merged company. And in some cases this led to rebellions by shareholders concerned not to sell independence too cheaply.

The possibility of bids also profoundly affected managements in firms whose independence was never challenged. The essence of a successful take-over was obtaining the backing of a majority of shareholders' votes. Hitherto, perhaps in the majority of quoted companies, fragmentation of shareholdings had left the actual control of companies in the hands of professional managers who might have little incentive to pursue profits where this conflicted with personal interests. The possibility of take-overs completely changed this situation: all firms, both potential bidders and potential victims, became more actively concerned with maintaining shareholder goodwill as reflected in the price of the company's shares.

On the other hand, there was a certain capriciousness about many of the take-overs that actually occurred. Decisions were made by persons (that is, shareholders) who had a very limited appreciation of the positive gains from the merger — as often on the basis of dissatisfaction with the existing management as from any well-founded view that the business would be better run as part of the larger organization implied in the bid. Indeed, in the case of some mergers, especially contested mergers, the bidding companies themselves were often in very great ignorance of the problems that subsequent integration of the business taken-over would bring. Moreover, in the short run, a bid against opposition involved the mounting of public campaigns by both sides. 'Victory' tended to be almost an end itself, especially for the professional advisers hired for the occasion, diverting attention from the real values and problems of subsequent integration.

These disadvantages were perhaps most manifest in the case of the financial entrepreneurs and the conglomerate empires they created. In theory they could have operated beneficially in effectively switching capital and managerial resources to the points where it could be most effectively used; and there were doubtless some cases where the tough discipline they introduced eliminated ineffective branch management. They may also, in ruthlessly eliminating loss-making businesses, have contributed to a greater mobility of the country's resources. Nevertheless, their own concern with maintaining and enhancing their Stock Exchange ratings made them excessively concerned with appearances: with revisions of accounting procedures to 'improve' their apparent profits or assets; with a maximization of visible profit within the short term horizon that was not necessarily consistent with long term profitable development. Nor were the skills, experience, or personal qualities that had brought success in the financial arena of the take-over battle the same, or necessarily very consistent with, those required for the management of business. Ruthless weeders are not necessarily good gardeners. In some cases the ventures ignominiously collapsed; and though many survived, none was an outstanding success. More generally, mergers in this period often disappointed those who undertook them, causing disruption to the constituent firms without obtaining many of the gains expected from integration. Size without thorough technical integration could not obtain the economies of scale. On the other hand, merging had considerable costs, both in its direct costs (for example, changing names) but also in the disruption and uncertainty it could bring that required considerable managerial effort and skill to avoid.

Financial Institutions

The most important group of financial institutions may be called the 'professional savers' — the insurance companies and the pension funds, institutions whose primary role was to find assets in which to invest the savings being made from their incomes by individuals or by employers acting for their employees. The flow of such funds was increasing through time, primarily reflecting increasing provision for old age, particularly through schemes organized by employers. Traditionally these institutions had held very much the larger part of their assets in the form of government securities, or as loans or mortgages with fixed interest and a prior charge on business. But in the post-war period this policy was

Table 5.1 Total holdings of financial institutions 1938–72 (£ millions)

	1938	1952	1962	1972
Building Society Assets	759	1478	3815	15246
Insurance companies	1740	4000	8180	22230
Pension funds	500	1250	4180	12010
Investment companies	310	580	2360	7520
Unit Trusts	80	100	260	2550
Total	3389	7408	18715	58556
Total at 1972 prices	16623	15291	30107	58556

Source: S. J. Prais, *The Evolution of Giant Firms in Britain* (Cambridge, 1976)

modified as the institutions sought security against inflation in the form of 'real' assets — property and the ordinary shares of companies — although it remained the case that the institutions continued to hold and acquire a fairly high proportion of fixed interest stocks. Insurance Companies which had no more than 3 per cent of their assets in ordinary shares before 1914 and 10 per cent in 1938 had 23 per cent in 1957 and 42 per cent in 1973.

Other personal savings were mainly lent to Building Societies (thence to finance other persons' house building) or to the Government as 'National Savings'; but from time to time from the late fifties quite large amounts were invested in Unit Trusts — which grew quite rapidly as professional investors who acted on behalf of the small saver who had a desire to invest in equities, but lacked either the knowledge of particular shares or a sufficiently large fortune to hold a widely spread portfolio. At the same time there seems to have been a considerable selling of shares by private individuals, presumably reflecting a running-down of their savings by the wealthy either to supplement income or to pay capital taxes.

Purchases of ordinary shares and of industrial debentures by savings institutions contributed significantly to the capital needs of industry. The contribution is more important than statistics sometimes suggest, because the statistics usually present the net inflow of finance as a percentage of gross capital formation — which includes both the investment needed to make good 'capital consumption' and that needed to finance the increased monetary value of stocks in an era of inflation. Moreover, even where the purchases of shares by institutions were having the effect of enabling the former holders of these shares to dissave, it would quite often be the case that this was enabling owners of small and medium businesses to extricate themselves without running down the capital employed in the business.

As a result of their share purchases, the institutions became the owners of increasing proportions of companies; their holdings of the ordinary shares of companies rose from 18 per cent in 1957 to about 50 per cent in 1975. This aggregate implies quite large holdings by individual institutions, and since institutions, unlike small private shareholders, might be expected to be in touch with one another, their holdings constituted significant blocks in almost every company. The institutions were very cautious in exercising their power directly, but their preferences were very important in take-over battles, and their opinions about the relative attractiveness of companies determined whether or not companies had high or low share prices — which in turn affected the companies' capacity for acquiring other companies or defending themselves.

These institutional holdings were themselves in the control of professional managers. These managers had strong interests in the flow of returns to bolster the visible balances of their own institutions, and consequently they had a preference for companies distributing high proportions of their earnings. Where their own performance was judged by the market value of the portfolio they had purchased, they had an immediate and continual interest in share prices, particularly in the case of Unit Trusts which attracted their unit-holders by publicity about relative performance. It also seems possible that like so many professional managers of other types of business they were unwilling to take risks unless they saw other institutions taking similar decisions.

Such behaviour must surely explain the extent of the fluctuations that occurred in Stock Exchange prices, even before the 1973–4 crisis. It is surprising that a market dominated by professionals should have fluctuated in the fifties and sixties at least as much as it had between the wars. In turn, the considerable fluctuations led to a concern with 'marketability': to the individual shareholder shares in a larger company were more attractive because he thought he was more likely to be able to sell his holding without disturbing the price. This factor tended to enhance the price of the shares of larger companies and may have contributed to the take-over movement.

A second group of institutions to be characterized as 'advisers' was represented primarily by the merchant banks (although, of course, they were also important borrowers and lenders of funds). These were important in providing advice both to savers (or more usually to the institutions which had received the savings) and to business borrowers. The advice to the latter might be about the implications for finance of the taxation system (the high levels of taxation and the rapid rate of change in its rates had increased the importance of this); about the advantageous employment of temporary balances (important in a world of high interest rates); about international financial arrangements; and about how take-over bids might be made or resisted.

It is difficult not to get the impression that in all this companies were being led into spending time reforming their structure, cultivating their 'image', and arranging their affairs to take maximum advantage of the financial world (and of the environment created by government finance) at the expense of their real business. Thus from the mid-fifties onwards, managements became increasingly conscious of their shareholders' potential power, and particularly of the interest of institutional shareholders in the distribution of profits as dividends. In turn, the increased distribution of dividends, together with a falling rate of profit, somewhat increased the need to finance investment by borrowing and by issues of shares — a need which made firms still more conscious of a need to have an acceptable reputation in the City of London.

At the same time their increasing size and their growing range of activities compelled most large firms to organize themselves on a divisional basis. Day-to-day operations and the formulation of many investment proposals were the responsibility of several specialist autonomous divisions, leaving to the main board of directors the responsibility for choosing from amongst the investment proposals put up to them by the divisions, and for choosing the senior managers of the divisions. By 1970, 72 of the 100 largest firms in Britain had a divisional organization, compared with only 13 in 1950. In both choosing investments and appraising success the central board had some resemblance to a financial institution dealing with independent firms, making judgments primarily in terms of profitability. The resemblance in most cases was limited; for despite their diversification most businesses had a limited range of activities, and within this range central management had a range of relevant knowledge and experience that gave it a potential for direct control most unlikely to exist in a financial institution.

Government policy, industrial structure, and competition

Until 1948 there was no legal or administrative restraint on restrictive agreements between firms to avoid price competition or on the use by individual firms of monopoly power. This contrasted with the United States, where there was prohibition of a wide variety of restrictive practices, and power to prevent the formation of monopolies. In 1948 the Monopolies and Restrictive Practices Commission was established to investigate individual cases and suggest appropriate remedies. The Commission form was an expression of uncertainty, or conflict of opinion, whether prohibition of monopoly might not damage efficient firms and make unattainable the economies of scale, given the size of the British market.

The major product of the 1948 Commission was a general report on restrictive practices, for which there seemed little defence in the post-war world. This lead to the Restrictive Practices Act of 1956 which made void a wide range of agreements unless a case satisfying specified conditions could be made to a Restrictive Practices Court. The early judgements of the Court, however, set harsh precedents, and most restrictive practices that depended on agreements between firms were abandoned by the early 1960s. Though some agreements had ceased to function before they were abandoned, and in other cases alternative forms of mutual restraint of competition evolved, there were many cases where the ending of agreements increased the degree of competition, sometimes to the extent of forcing firms to merge. Resale Price Maintenance, the enforcement by a manufacturer of a schedule of prices on his distributors (especially retail distributors), survived the 1956 Act, but was made registrable, subject to similar scrutiny by the Court, and, with few exceptions, was discontinued by an Act of 1964.

Meanwhile, the 1948 Commission confined its attentions to situations where single firms or small groups dominated the production of particular goods. A great deal of information was made public, and this in itself may have had some effect in modifying their practices. But in many cases no drastic recommendations were made, and in others such recommendations that were made were not accepted by the government. In 1965 the Commission's powers were extended to consider the desirability of proposed mergers (hitherto it had considered products and markets rather than firms as a whole). It made some important recommendations (notably against the mergers proposed between Barclays and Lloyds Banks and between Rank and De La Rue) but its general effectiveness was limited by the government's unwillingness to refer many cases to it. Moreover, in the absence of firm guidelines comparable to those regulating restrictive practices, the Commission found itself involved in basing judgements on predictions about future consequences, matters on which it either had to give the benefit of considerable doubt to the applicant companies or on which its verdicts were likely to seem intolerably arbitrary.

In official thinking the disadvantages of size were thought to lie entirely in the potential power to oppress customers, whilst the possibility that mergers might lead to less efficient firms was ignored. In the mid-sixties there was indeed a rather uncritial acceptance of the advantages of size. In 1966 the Labour Government established the Industrial Reconstruction Corporation to promote 're-structuring'. Logically it had a role, for there could well be situations in industries where the process by which one individual firm takes over others in succession could not unlock the potentialities for rationalization. But in other cases where it intervened, the logic seems to have been rather different, and to have depended on the notion (rather curious under a government of the left) that there was a rather limited body of managerial talent on whom an indefinite amount of responsibility could be placed without detracting from its efficiency. This was disastrous in the case of British Leyland, where a successful producer of buses and lorries, that had itself been expanding somewhat recklessly into car production, was presented with the accumulated problems of a different type of business.

Throughout the whole period there was an official disposition to assume that generally the British economy was hampered by having firms and plants that were too small — an assumption that may have been derived from the immediate post-war period when almost all comparisons were made with the United States, for it had no factual basis in comparisons with European countries; by the 1960s firms and plants in Britain seem to have been very much the same size as in Germany and larger than in other countries.

There can be no doubt that the effect of many mergers was to make competition between companies less intense than it would otherwise have been. Even mergers that involved diversification were often supplemented by less-publicized changes in which individual subsidiaries were resold, normally to firms in the same industry. In almost every type of production there were increases in the share of output for which the larger firms were responsible; and in some cases, for example, textiles, where production was not very concentrated at the start of the period, these increases were large. It would however be wrong to suppose that the intensity of competition fell to the extent indicated by indices of concentration; for other factors were operating to increase competition. From outside the country the reduction of tariffs and communication costs enormously increased the number of potential suppliers of manufactured goods. Faced with such competition there would have been little point in British manufacturers attempting to maintain restrictive agreements even if the Restrictive Practices Act of 1956 had not been passed. There were some sectors, for example the production of building materials and construction itself, which remained insulated from foreign competition by high transport costs. Even here the reduction within the country of road transport costs increased the number of potential suppliers at particular places.

Nor should all growth be seen as increasing monopoly power to be used at the expense of the final consumer. The growth of the great retailers created purchasers whose size and ability to search world-wide for suppliers enabled them to obtain good prices and quality, advantages which were almost entirely transmitted to the final customer by fierce competition between the retailers. In part competition in the retail trade was just an extreme example of a more general phenomenon: the fact that firms' financial scale had generally grown more quickly than the minimum scale required to operate in particular markets; and the fact that they were already accustomed to operating in several markets gave them an ability to switch resources into new fields they saw as being profitable.

In the first decade after the War, restrictive agreements and the practice of Resale Price Maintenance continued the inter-war situation where producers avoided competition between one another in terms of price, and distributive outlets also avoided price competition. But over the next twenty years the amount of price competition increased considerably, in part because of the virtual abolition of collective R.P.M. by the 1956 Restrictive Practices Act and of individual R.P.M. by the 1964 Resale Price Maintenance Act, but perhaps mainly because a sufficient number of retailers saw price competition as a way of increasing their share of business.

It is always difficult to say how much price competition there is when manufacturers make products that are similar but not identical. In this period manufacturers often sought success by introducing new products on which they hoped for high profit margins rather than by seeking to produce existing products at lower prices. But it was also a world in which consumers naturally preferred to spend part of their increased incomes on better rather than more goods; and manufacturers themselves in their purchases found it economic to pay premium prices for machines and materials that directly or indirectly saved labour. That many 'new' products subsequently seemed unimaginative variations should probably be seen as a natural consequence of a search by trial and error in a world where consumers' requirements are very imperfectly known — a search conducted by managers of varying inspiration and competence, rather than as a consequence of conspiracy against the consumer.

There were many cases, notoriously detergents, where competition between a small number of firms took the form of a level of advertising that it is difficult for a detached observer not to think wasteful. (Though since advertising itself had valuable by-products like television, newspapers, and the sponsoring of sports events it is difficult to say quite how large the net social cost was). It seems most plausible to see such expenditures as a type of continuous oligopolistic warfare in which the generals on either side sought to gain, or regain, market shares — sometimes by product innovation, and sometimes by special offers, as well as by advertising. They were contests by professional managements unduly conscious of their rights to market shares and unduly confident in their capacities to win the next offensive. The notion that the two sides were not really fighting but were in tacit collusion, and that their shots were not aimed at one another but scattered at random to deter other firms from entering the battlefield seems less plausible.

Advertising as such, after a sharp revival from the low level to which it had fallen during the War, was no higher in the 1960s than between the Wars (2 per cent of G.D.P.). Any apparent increase in the amounts of advertising must be explicable as a consequence of greater efficiency of delivery through television and mass-circulation newspapers. There are no statistics about other types of marketing expenditure, which are difficult to separate from the central activities of firms. Any assumption that they rose should be tempered by the consideration that economy of distribution expenditure motivated many mergers; and that the success of many retailers depended on sales of 'own brands' on which promotional expenditure was cut to a minimum.

Small companies

The proportion of net manufacturing output produced by firms with less than 200 employees fell from 35 per cent in 1935 to 16 per cent in 1963. There was also a decline in the relative importance of small businesses in every other sector: retailing, construction, catering, vehicle distribution and repair, and other miscellaneous services.

The environment that produced this decline was not totally hostile to the prosperity of small firms. Many businesses were established and grew very rapidly. Often such small businesses were successful in introducing new products well designed to meet a need not noticed by larger companies. It must, however, be observed that such growth often ended in the firm moving out of the small category, and frequently in the firm being taken-over. And it is difficult for someone in 1979 to see how far success stories that began in the 1940s and 1950s were being matched by firms born in the 1960s. Moreover, among the small businesses surviving in the seventies it is difficult to say how many had a substantial degree of independence. In many circumstances it was convenient for large companies to sub-contract rather than produce all their own components; or they might choose to sell their products, or services, through nominally independent 'franchised' retailers; in the extreme a stone quarry might devise a scheme to enable its drivers to own their own lorries. How clearly distinct, in practice, were such arrangements from systems where managers, or even rank-and-file employees, were given substantial incentives tied to the profitability of the business they handled? Legal independence did not preclude substantial dependence in practice.

We have discussed on page 70 some of the factors contributing to the decline of small businesses. It is difficult to see any of them, other than the operation of highly progressive taxation on wealthy owners, as the product of government policy rather than the natural environment — and at all times there was some mitigation of the full rigours of taxation.

In the 1970s, after so many had gone, it became fashionable to regret the departure of small firms. The social basis of this view is understandable. Economically it is more questionable, for it depends on assuming that all small firms would have had the characteristics of those still surviving: agility and adaptability to earn a living from the opportunities neglected by (or unsuitable for) giants, and in so doing, providing for neglected needs. But it could be argued that a factor contributing to impeding growth in productivity earlier in the century was the tying up of resources of men and capital in small family units that had lost the drive that had established them and which, protected by the Limited Liability Acts, could continue to enjoy the active management of their businesses at relatively low risk.

Public enterprise

Under the Labour government of 1945–51, the coal industry, the larger part of the steel industry, the airlines, long-distance road haulage, electricity, gas and the railways were 'nationalized'. Many electricity and gas producers were already in public ownership, and all, like the railways, were subject to detailed regulation, long thought necessary to prevent public utilities exploiting their monopoly powers. In the cases of electricity and gas the purpose of nationalization was primarily to reap economies of production

Table 5.2 The Nationalized industries

	1951	1964	1975
As percentages of G.D.P.			
Net Value Added	10·4	10·1	11·7
Gross Trading Surplus	2·0	3·2	3·3
Net Trading Surplus	0·2	0·8	0·1
Investment as percentage of all U.K. investment.	18·7	19·7	19·0

that were thought to stem from national rather than local organization. In the case of the railways it was thought that there were similar economies, though in addition nationalization was seen by some as part of a wider scheme of transport 'integration'. This wider intention was not carried out: at the stage of nationalization the Labour government limited itself to long-distance road haulage and did not persist in an attempt to limit the right of firms to carry their own goods; and subsequently a large part of the long-distance industry was resold by Conservative governments to private enterprise. The airlines were a sector where it was thought that national prestige required large investment, but where experience suggested that private enterprise would not fill this role spontaneously without substantial subsidies. Coal had been, overall, a declining industry, where widespread unprofitability had already required publicly sponsored restriction of output in 1931, where labour relations were generally poor, and where the labourforce demanded nationalization. The producers of bulk steel had already been cartelized behind a high protective wall in the 1930s. At the time steel was first nationalized (1949) it is difficult to discern an economic motive other than a mystique deriving from its central importance in an earlier stage of industrialization, as part of 'the commanding heights of capitalism'. Subsequently, before re-nationalization in 1967, technical change had made the industry more obviously in need of further concentration.

The above account is brief. It is also to some extent imaginative, for, despite the important part that nationalization played in the Labour Party's programme and despite the priority of time and effort given to it by the Labour government in 1945–51, there was relatively little coherent discussion of the economics of nationalization. Equally important, there was relatively little discussion of the economic guidelines to be followed by the nationalized enterprises other than that they were expected to break even, 'taking one year with another', and, in some cases, inherited restrictions designed to prevent monopolistic exploitation of customers.

As it turned out the industries had much less monopolistic power than may have been expected. Apart from the ability of private firms to generate electricity for their own consumption, there was competition in the fuel sector because no attempt was made to restrain competition between the three nationalized industries themselves, made keener by the revival of gas in the 1960s on the basis of oil conversion and North Sea discoveries, and because of competition from fuel oil. Similarly, in transport, the monopoly position of the railways largely disappeared — except for some London commuters. Electricity did retain its position as effectively the only supplier of lighting and of electromotive power for most users. But it was perhaps the Post Office, in its control of communication by both post and telephone, that most closely conformed to the nineteenth-century picture of a monopolist public utility oppressing its customers not so much by rapacious profit-making as by neglect of their preferences for its own bureaucratic convenience.

There was a tendency among a large part of the public to assume that industries that had been nationalized were *ipso facto* 'social services' with outputs to which everyone was entitled on favourable terms. This opinion tended to be reinforced by an economic theory that price should be fixed at 'marginal cost' which it was assumed in the case of public utilities would often involve selling at a loss. Both arguments were difficult to sustain in relation to the industries actually nationalized. With few exceptions the relevant marginal cost of production was higher than average cost, and the application of the economic theory would have involved the earning of higher profits rather than the incurring of losses. Part of the output may have been for uses that were 'socially essential' — but it was equally true that consumption of the output differed greatly between individuals, the output of some (for example, air and rail travel) being proportionately more important for the rich than for the poor. Alternatively the outputs themselves constituted inputs to all other industry. This might justify calling them basic, but it did not constitute a case for encouraging their greater use by the charging of low prices.

A characteristic of the nationalized industries was that they were great and intensive users of capital (absorbing between 20 and 25 per cent of Domestic Capital Formation by contrast with the 10 per cent of G.D.P. for which they were responsible). This was mainly financed by borrowing, and since they were nationalized the industries borrowed on terms that related to the government's own borrowing. In common with that borrowing, the rate of interest actually paid seldom reflected the true 'opportunity cost' of the real resources required for capital investment; and furthermore there was no additional premium for the real risks involved in the actual decisions of the industries. Since in many cases there were technical alternatives involving the spending of more or less capital or even restriction of output, there was a general tendency for the nationalized industries to make excessive demands for capital. At times, particularly in the case of the electricity industry in the 1950s, where it was thought impolitic to risk having to restrict supply, these demands were met with too little question. In other cases, approval of investment was withheld and the success of an industry's board in obtaining its requirements was as much a matter of political lobbying as of rational calculation.

Inflationary conditions affected the industries in two ways. Firstly, and this particularly applies to the period up to the onset of rapid inflation in the 1970s, borrowing at relatively low rates of interest and accounting on a historic cost principle in capital-intensive industries tended to understate their true costs, and either overstate profits or understate losses; leading perhaps in the case of electricity to an excessive expansion of demand induced by prices which were too low. Secondly, particularly in the seventies, but also on occasion before, ministers used their direct influence to keep prices down to make a visible contribution either to holding down the cost of living in the case of transport and fuel, or maintaining 'export competitiveness' in the case of steel. Such intervention necessarily blurred the obligation upon managers to cover their costs, and in turn brought into question whether the industries were dependent on their revenue and consequently part of the 'market sector', or whether they were to become like other public bodies.

It must be remembered that for some supporters the primary purpose of nationalization had been to liberate industries from economic forces, technical gains from national integration being no more than convenient supporting arguments. Thus coal miners saw nationalization as freeing them from the effects of price competition between different pits and different areas, and pushed for equalization of wages despite the great differences in productivity between areas. It was taken for granted that the industry should be looked at as a whole with consistently unprofitable pits being supported by the surpluses of others. When demand fell drastically and large losses threatened, it was still not accepted that closures should be related to unprofitability regardless of area.

Similarly, railways and steel were hindered in their pursuit of efficiency by a need to consider the interests of their large labour-forces, particularly those in Scotland and Wales, which saw themselves threatened by labour-saving changes and by concentration of the industry on its most profitable branches. The constraints were partly those of direct industrial sanctions, the effectiveness of which was increased rather than reduced by the unified ownership of the industry, but also those of political intervention from the regions affected.

No such problems afflicted the electricity industry, which followed fifteen years of apparent success in improving efficiency with three considerable failures: an excessive expansion of capacity — which in a capital-intensive industry was very costly; a technical failure to achieve further economies by increasing the scale of generating equipment; and a failure to obtain the economies expected from the gas-cooled atomic reactors. To a considerable extent the blame for the failures lay with the government which pushed the C.E.G.B. (Central Electricity Generating Board) into being too adventurous, and with the construction industry which required such long periods for construction and increased the hazards of demand forecasting. There were, nevertheless, probably two internal faults: a naïve acceptance that a rapid growth of demand was a permament feature of the electricity industry; and an inexplicable failure to test new developments before standardizing them.

The importance of multi-national firms for the United Kingdom economy

Britain's role in the pre-1914 world as an exporter of capital and enterprise had led to the establishment of companies based in the U.K. whose operations were almost entirely overseas and concerned with the production of materials: wool, tea, cocoa, and rubber; gold and other metals; and oil. In the case of minerals and oil, comparatively small initial investments had been the seed of enterprises that by re-investment of large returns and some amalgamations were half-a-century later giants by national and international standards — notably British Petroleum and Shell, Anglo-American Corporation and other gold companies, and Rio Tinto Zinc.

The post-war boom in primary products, particularly the very rapid increase in world consumption of petroleum, must have brought very high profits to these companies and made the balance-of-payments position of Britain less critical than it would otherwise have been. From the early 1950s the growth of such companies was increasingly subject to political constraints, particularly in countries that had either recently achieved legal independence or wished to assert an independence that previously had in practice been limited (for example, most of the Middle East); but the companies themselves retained considerable bargaining power because of their control of market outlets, their expertise in prospecting, and their ability to obtain the large amounts of capital necessary to make some mineral developments viable. Both the latter factors reflected the exhaustion in the century after 1870 of many of the most easily accessible deposits.

The oil companies, even after the fall in prices in the fifties and sixties caused by the competition of new producers, were able to finance a large part of their operations. In other areas of mineral extraction there continued to be a great deal of British based enterprise; but limitations on the ability to obtain capital in the United Kingdom led to a considerable increase in foreign shareholdings. In many cases, because of the disadvantages of U.K. taxation for non-residents, and because of nationalistic sentiment, this was followed by an emigration of the companies to centres nearer their operations in South Africa, Australia, Canada, and Singapore. Until the discoveries of North Sea gas and oil in the late 1960s, there was no inward flow of foreign capital in the extractive industries, though many oil companies invested in large refineries in the United Kingdom both because of its convenient situation and because of favourable tax treatment that was obtained on profits.

In many ways the U.K.-based multi-nationals producing materials were quite separate from the U.K. domestic economy. But many possessed important industrial plants in the U.K., for example, petro-chemicals; and indeed in some cases (Unilever) manufacturing was their primary interest. Their personnel moved between one type of branch and another disseminating managerial style, and their importance as clients contributed to the perpetuation of an internationalist ideology among British financial institutions. Not least, their importance for the balance-of-payments made more difficult the formulation by the government of clear-cut policies towards multi-nationals.

Manufacturer multi-nationals constituted a second more numerous type that, in the world as a whole, was more important than the raw material producers. These were firms that, having established themselves as manufacturers in one country, at a certain point in their development decided to establish overseas branches — in some cases the branches would be doing no more than assisting the sale of goods exported from the original base, but frequently they would develop into assemblers of parts and full-scale manufacturers. Several factors accelerated these developments in the third quarter of the century. An increasing proportion of goods required special local service subsequent to sale (for example, the spares, supplementary accessories, up-dating modifications, and instructions to users, required to support the sale of computers) and made it desirable to control the sale and delivery of products overseas rather than rely on merchants. In some cases where transportation costs were high it made obvious sense to produce nearer to the final consumer, a consideration reinforced if artificial factors like tariffs or government purchasing policies favoured local suppliers.

In other cases difference in labour cost made it more advantageous to produce overseas even for third markets — a factor important in the emigration of U.S. enterprise. Not least important was the possibility of maintaining fairly close control because of the cheapening of telephonic communication and the ability of managers to visit branches by air.

Such multi-nationals were already well-established before 1939: Ford had been in Britain for a quarter of a century, Singer for more than half. A survey in 1965 showed that two-thirds of overseas investment in the U.K. belonged to companies that had established themselves in the U.K. before 1945. But the relative importance of foreign multi-nationals in U.K. production increased considerably in the post-war period. By 1963 (for which the first accurate statistics are available) they accounted for 10 per cent of the output of manufacturing and 7 per cent of the employment — probably double the proportions of 1953, and possibly as much as four or five times the proportions in 1939. By 1968 they accounted for 14 per cent of output and 10 per cent of employment. About three-quarters of the investment came from North America.

In the early post-war period an important attraction may have been a desire to get behind the barrier to imports constituted by the high British tariff and by controls on imports (as well as to share the advantages which Imperial Preference gave British exporters in the Commonwealth). But the continued inward investment, together with the fact that many overseas subsidiaries were quite large exporters from the U.K., suggests that the U.K. was seen as a good manufacturing base with relatively cheap labour, a wide range of skills, attractive fiscal treatment of investment, and, for Americans, the attraction of speaking English. For U.S. investors the attractions of the U.K. decreased in the 1970s. In 1976 less than 13 per cent of the U.S. capital stock employed in manufacturing was in the U.K., compared with about 16 per cent in the 1960s; and the rate of return which had exceeded 15 per cent in the 1950s and generally exceeded 10 per cent in the 1960s, fell to 5·4 per cent in 1976.

Britain was also the home base of large manufacturing multi-nationals, and there was a substantial flow of outward investment. The real flow was exaggerated by statistics which failed to make proper allowance for inflation; but it was nevertheless quite large when compared with the outflow from Germany. To a considerable extent this is to be explained as a natural consequence of the longer establishment of British firms overseas, and their ploughing back of the profits of the established subsidiaries. But, at least in some years, there can be little doubt that investment overseas had some risk-spreading attractions and that these risks included the political risks attached to capital in the U.K. In consequence, some of the investment overseas was not made because of the positive attraction of good investment opportunities, and (for example in Canada in the mid-fifties) it proved to have a very low return.

There was much concern about multi-nationals; indeed in the late 1960s there were enquiries into both outward investment (Reddaway) and inward investment (Steuer). The concern was understandable. There was the bewildering complexity of the effect of multi-nationals on the balance-of-payments. There were fiscal problems of defining the profits earned in the country and therefore subject to taxation, with the suspicion that companies took advantage of any available accounting ambiguity to show their profits as being earned overseas. But above all there was the simple ability of multi-nationals to switch their operations and the employment they gave between countries. In dealing with the multi-nationals, therefore, governments found their coercive power to be inadequate and were pushed into persuasion and even supplication. In short, multi-nationals were an affront to governments and to national sovereignty. But this does not imply that their existence, any more than that of the Catholic Church in the Middle Ages, necessarily operated to the disadvantage of all the inhabitants of the kingdom, because it challenged the supremacy of their government.

6 The labour market

Changes in labour supply

Table 6.1 Participation Rates: (percentages of various categories of the population who were actively employed)

		1931	1951	1961	1971
Male and Female	15–19	77·6	81·3	72·9	58·4
Married Women	25–34	13·2	24·4	29·5	38·4
	35–44	10·1	25·7	36·4	54·2
	45–54	8·5	23·7	35·3	56·8
	55–59	7·0	15·6	26·0	45·1
Men	20–24	97·2	94·9	93·2	90·3
	60–64	87·6	87·7	91·0	86·6
	65–69	65·4	47·7	39·9	30·5

Note: The table includes only those important groups where there were large changes in participation. For most of the male population, and for single females, the changes were much smaller.

We saw earlier that the total numbers in the labour-force increased because greater participation by married women swamped a reduced participation by other parts of the population, and that hours of work per year fell, but hours of work per week fell only slightly. Subject to the availability of work, all these changes were the consequence of economic choices made by individuals, or individual families, for except in wartime nobody was compelled to work.

The decline in participation by the young was a consequence of the increases in the school leaving age, together with the extension of higher education. Some part of this, particularly the support by parents of children in the 16–18 range, may have reflected higher incomes, but a great deal was the consequence of wide availability of relatively generous grants (by international standards) and the provision from the early 1960s onwards of a great many more places in universities and polytechnics.

The elderly had less need to work. Old Age Pensions were extended by the National Insurance Act 1946 to cover eventually all who retired. Though the real value of pensions was continuously eroded by inflation, pension rates were increased so that, over the whole period, their real worth increased absolutely and kept pace with the earnings of the employed. Moreover, as time went on, an increasing number of those retiring benefited from private superannuation schemes, while pensioners with no other sources of income were automatically granted Supplementary Benefit. But the dividing line between 'voluntary' and 'involuntary' retirement is difficult to define and impossible to observe; it cannot be assumed that all the elderly who ceased to work did so willingly. It would probably have been more difficult for employers to find suitable jobs for the same proportion of the population over 65, because of the increasing proportion of the population of that age. But the reduction in employment went further, and the actual number of over-65s employed declined.

Three types of organizational factor seem responsible for this. First, the unwillingness of unions to include in their agreements with employers lower-paid employments for the elderly; and their insistence that, in cases where redundancy was required, those at or near to the formal retirement age should be first to go. Second, an increasing proportion of retirements were from non-manual employments, where salaries tended to increase with age. This produced a situation where, especially if there was a decline in efficiency towards the retiring age, the salaries paid were increasingly out of line with the actual productivity of the individual; alternatively, where salaries were associated with movement up a hierarchy, the need to provide advancement for the young required the regular retirement of the elderly. Third, these factors were likely to be more important for large organizations, which have need for simple uniform rules. Whether, in addition to these organizational factors, the increasing pace of technical change was a factor is not clear, for while the elderly may be less adaptable than the young to changing techniques, they may not be much less adaptable than the middle-aged.

One important factor in the increased employment of women was the removal of institutional barriers during the War; for example, against the employment of female bus conductors, or against married women teachers. But the fact that such barriers were not re-erected after the Second War, as they had been after the First, must itself be explained by the continuation of full employment. More generally, for twenty years, the high demand for labour made employers more willing to consider the employment of women, and unions more willing to accept it. At the same time the number of jobs at which women were at no physical disadvantage increased, most obviously in offices but also in many light branches of manufacturing. Indeed in many cases a labour-force with a high proportion of women was attractive to employers: partly because until the Equal Pay Act of 1968 began to operate in the 1970s, their wages were lower; but also because the greater frequency with which they changed, or ceased, employment made them less concerned with protecting their long term position by strong union organization. We must also notice that government policy in directing industry to the depressed areas often introduced light industry, which provided employment for women in areas where it had not previously been available.

Government policy was to remove obstacles to the employment of married women. It was one factor leading to the introduction of universally available school lunches in wartime. In 1941 married women were given an allowance to be set against income tax liability—and during the next thirty-five years this was the only allowance that was fully revised to keep pace with inflation.

But all cannot be explained in terms of demand. Indeed, after the War women's earnings did not increase, relative to those of men, until after the Equal Pay Act of 1968 (see p. 106); and this continued cheapness of female labour requires some explanation. The obvious explanation was an increased desire by women to work. No doubt to some extent this was a non-economic phenomenon, with employment providing attractions other than wage packets. In so far as there is an economic explanation, it must lie in the development of a greater range of consumer goods at accessible prices. One effect was simply to raise the level of material aspirations. There are also many cases where the development of consumer products released the time and energy of wives from their household tasks — not only durable 'capital' goods like washing machines, dish-washers, and central heating, but also cooked and prepared foods, and easy-care clothes. Similarly, there were changes in the location and nature of retailing to permit shopping near to work and time-economizing shopping. Of course, these changes in goods and organization are not all to be seen as 'exogenous' factors; they in turn were to a large extent responses to market opportunities presented by the purchasing power and the needs of employed married women. But not all changes were such a response, for in some cases new products enabled the housewife to perform for herself services which she could previously have purchased (for example, washing-machines were substitutes for laundries) — though substitution in this direction was much greater in the case of men's activities, like house painting.

In formal economic terms the change that occurred could be described as a shift in the boundary between the household and the market economies, with the household offering more labour to the market and replacing internal household activities with goods and services provided by the market. In most cases the household was a family, not an individual. While the increased supply of labour by women was too widespread a phenomenon to be associated with actual decline of husbands' earnings, it seems significant that the extent of married women's employment was distinctly higher than in other developed countries — reflecting perhaps aspirations to material standards that were not matched by productivity. Moreover, the increased female participation needs to be seen in conjunction with the perceptible decline in hours worked by male members of the labour-force.

It would be too simple to see this change merely as a substitution of 'leisure' for 'work' — though that is no doubt quite a large part of it. For how was the time spent? In so far as it was spent on decorating houses, servicing cars, cultivating gardens, it was providing 'household' substitutes for services that might have been purchased (and which would, had they been purchased, have been added to the G.D.P.) — that is, movement in the opposite direction to the effect of housewives taking employment.

One consequence of a more equal distribution of incomes was the greater-than-average rise in price of labour-intensive services like house-decoration. This changed the relative advantage of working in order to employ a decorator compared with Do-It-Yourself. The shift was made greater by the effect of high levels of taxation. Paying 40 per cent income tax and national insurance on marginal income, a family needed to earn £1.66 for each £1 paid to a decorator. With the introduction of V.A.T. in 1973 the earnings required were increased to £1.83.

But in adducing all these aspects of life in the third quarter of the twentieth century, we should not neglect the abiding proposition that it is likely that, when ability to earn more real income per hour increases, fewer hours of labour will be supplied because 'leisure' is a good. Since the middle of the nineteenth century, increases in real income had been accompanied by very considerable falls in the length of the working week and some increase in holidays, and perhaps what needs to be explained about the whole period 1937 –75 is why the reduction in hours was not greater. This must reflect one or both of two fundamental factors: with previous reductions in hours of work and improved working conditions, work itself was no longer so onerous; and the availability of new types of goods on which to spend incomes indirectly increased the attractiveness of employment.

The nature of employment

Changes in the terms and nature of employment are sometimes seen exclusively in political or social terms, as consequences of the achievement by unions, either through direct bargaining with employers or by their influence on government, of the evolving aspirations of the working class. We need, however, to consider the possibility that other factors have played some part — without necessarily being exclusive causes: the changing nature of work-tasks, the changing character of employment organizations, and the changing balance of supply and demand in the labour market.

Between 1931 and 1966, when the total occupied population rose by 17 per cent, the number of manual workers declined by 2 per cent, while the number of white-collar workers doubled. Some of this change reflected the decreased importance of sectors with a high proportion of manual workers, but it also reflected the increasing relative importance of white-collar labour in all sectors. Thus the proportion of white-collar workers in industry rose from 1/8th in 1931 to 1/6th in 1948, and to over 1/4 in 1966. Much of this

Table 6.2 Occupational distribution of working population (percentages)

	Men			Women		
	1931	1951	1971	1931	1951	1971
1. Self-employed and Higher Professions	**1·7**	**2·8**	**6·1**	**1·0**	**1·0**	**1·4**
2. Employers and Proprietors	**7·6**	**5·7**	**5·2**	**4·4**	**3·2**	**2·9**
3. White Collar	**19·3**	**23·1**	**29·9**	**26·5**	**41·6**	**52·7**
Managers & Administrators	*4·5*	*6·8*	*9·9*	*1·6*	*2·7*	*3·3*
Lower Professions & Techicians	*1·8*	*3·0*	*5·5*	*6·0*	*7·9*	*10·8*
Supervisors & Foremen	*2·0*	*3·3*	*4·5*	*0·4*	*1·1*	*1·2*
Clerical Workers	*5·1*	*6·0*	*6·1*	*10·3*	*20·3*	*28·0*
Salesmen & Shop Assistants	*5·9*	*4·0*	*3·9*	*8·2*	*9·6*	*9·4*
4. Manual	**71·4**	**68·4**	**58·8**	**68·1**	**54·2**	**43·0**
Skilled	*30·1*	*30·3*	*29·4*	*19·2*	*12·7*	*9·3*
Semi-skilled	*23·4*	*24·3*	*21·2*	*41·4*	*33·6*	*27·3*
Unskilled	*17·9*	*13·8*	*8·2*	*7·5*	*7·9*	*6·4*

Source: A. H. Halsey: *Change in British Society* (Oxford, 1978)

white-collar labour was employed on tasks that did not result in individually measurable output, did not bear a close relationship to the firm's current output, required a degree of willingness and of responsible care that could not be defined precisely in advance, and in many cases an accumulation of knowledge about the firm itself. Such labour was naturally more evenly employed and, quite apart from its attraction to the employee, the employer had considerable interest in employees staying with the business. Precise payments by results are an infeasible form of incentive, but prospects of promotion and accordance of seniority could be attractive — as could pensions.

Not all white-collar jobs had these characteristics (a roomful of girls checking football pools was not very different from one where they were sewing shirts) and conversely not all manual jobs lacked them. Indeed technical change, by on the one hand changing the worker's task to an observer of processes intervening only to correct abnormalities, and on the other making him the custodian of valuable pieces of fixed capital (where the damage possible from inattention might be very high) increased the value to the employer of careful attention, as opposed to simple manual effort, in many jobs. Despite this, output-related payment remained very important — and covered about 50 per cent of manual employments in the early 1960s.

Firms became much larger. With size went the development of bureaucracy and hierarchy, which in turn brought a concern amongst managers themselves that differentials should be 'fair and proper' both for themselves and for those working with them. This was tempered to some extent by the continued existence of a 'labour market' setting prices on particular jobs — and indeed superficial evidence of newspaper advertisements suggests a market with increasing activity. Nevertheless, in defining what a job was, the special circumstances peculiar to each firm left it some scope to create its own pattern. In public employment the scope was even greater.

But superimposed on all these considerations was the general situation in the labour market. From 1945 to 1965, some would say until 1975, there was full employment, with many types of labour in very short supply. This was a new experience for British employers, who in the past had normally been operating in a buyer's market in which they could take their pick and where, however considerate they may have been in their dealings with employees, the possibility of termination of employment remained a potent unspoken threat. A phenomenon associated with full employment was high labour turnover — individuals moving from job to job searching for something more suitable (perhaps in some cases to an excessive extent even from their own point of view). This was costly to employers because virtually all labour requires time to adapt itself to particular employments. Consequently both to attract and to keep labour, firms had to think about what they could offer apart from wages.

For many members of the labour-force, who were well enough paid for immediate wages not to be the only consideration, the attractiveness of an employment included the facilities offered, the security and prospects, and being treated fairly and decently. That is to put matters at an everyday level. It is also the case that post-war management doctrine was increasingly dominated by sociological considerations in its prescriptions; but whether this was a factor of widespread importance is difficult to determine.

The argument above is not to say that legislation was without effect. The Contracts of Employment Act 1963 pulled the practice of all employers towards the standards of the better managed firms, the Redundancy Payments Act of 1965 enforced a level of compensation that enlightened employers would have accepted, but not necessarily adopted in the form required, while the Trade Union and Labour Relations and the Employment Protection Acts of 1975 went far beyond what any employer could have thought to be 'enlightened self-interest' in the rights given to trade unions and the security given to all employment. In a slightly different sphere, the Equal Pay Act of 1968 removed discrepancies between the pay of men and women which market forces had done nothing to reduce for twenty years.

The economic significance of trade unions

Membership of trade unions increased from about 30 per cent of the labour-force in 1938 to 45 per cent in 1948. In part this was because of the expansion of industries, like engineering, where they were strong, and in part because of the rights they were given during the War to act against firms that did not recognize them. From 1948 to the mid-sixties membership drooped, because of a decline in the manpower in railways and mining, and because of the declining relative importance of manual employment. Subsequently, after 1968 there was a distinct upturn, and by 1976 membership exceeded 55 per cent. The upturn preceded the legislation of the mid-seventies which facilitated union recruitment, and must reflect a change in attitude amongst the labour-force to the benefits that they supposed membership could bring or to the dangers, including redundancy and accelerating inflation, from which they wished to be protected.

The economic effects of unionization in the United Kingdom is not a subject on which anybody has succeeded in making a convincing, simple, clear-cut judgement. In the event, it has never been possible to determine how far the betterment of their members' conditions was primarily a consequence of underlying favourable economic factors: the long period of full employment with excess demand for many types of manual labour; the effect of the long-term expansion of the educational system in increasing the supply of non-manual skills and reducing the supply of manual labour; and the very considerable increase in the number of employments that the mobility of the typical member of the labour-force enabled him to consider. On the whole the efforts of the unions were devoted to working through the market by collective bargaining and, even when they sought legislation, this was in many cases intended to improve their bargaining power rather than to supersede the market mechanism.

Some types of union activity can be categorized in economic analysis as making more perfect the operations of the labour market. Without unions, in these cases, employers would be what economists call monopsonists. That is they would be able to bargain with their individual employees with the advantage of more knowledge about an employee's worth to himself or to alternative employers than the employee himself has. Sometimes also employers, because of their individual importance in a neighbourhood or because of understandings with other employers, even have control over the prospects of their employees' alternative employment. In the twentieth century, the increasing proportion of the population in large conurbations and, even more important, the increased ability of the working population to travel long distances to work, enhanced during the fifties and sixties by the spread of car-ownership, very much reduced employers' monopsonistic power over employees whose skills were of a standard, and therefore of a relatively marketable, kind. It may also be that education had diminished the scope for exploitation based on ignorance. These factors could be important even where individual employers were very large — for large firms, though they may have monopolies in their products, do not necessarily have significant monopsonies in the purchase of standard types of labour.

On the other hand a great many, possibly an increasing proportion, of jobs involved the development of knowledge and skills not readily marketable; and here employees were necessarily in a weaker position (not necessarily unjustly, since acquiring the knowledge or skill may have involved no special virtue, effort, or intrinsic ability on their part). More generally many aspects of employment, particularly those offering prospects of promotion, seniority payments, and pensions, could be seen as baits used by employers to draw employees into situations in which they became more dependent. This is to take a sour view of arrangements that both employer and employee had often seen as mutually beneficial for the sort of reasons discussed in the previous section. But such a souring may account for the rapid development of non-manual unions in the 1970s among a part of the labour-force that came to see itself as vulnerable in comparison with the unionized labour-force in the competitive process of keeping up with inflation; and for whom the end of the rapid growth of employment had much reduced the prospects of promotion.

But though many unions may justify their existence in terms of employers' potential monopsony, their ambitions are not usually confined to seeking the rewards of a competitive market for their members. The case of the soccer players for whom it was sufficient to rid themselves of a standardized wage and to reduce the restrictions on their ability to transfer was quite untypical. Normally unions wished to obtain for their members either higher wages or greater security of employment than they feared a free market would provide. To achieve this they had three modes of action. They might obtain legislation: for example, establishing a board to set minimum wages, a device extended to the catering industry in 1943 but not one much favoured by unions, who naturally hoped for a more active institutional role for themselves; or decasualizing dock labour, establishing control of entry, and obtaining a monopoly of dock and related work. Secondly they might, for example, by apprenticeship regulations, seek to control entry into certain occupations, and to confine particular types of work to their members, thus creating or enhancing a market scarcity. It is not obvious that many new restrictions of this sort were created during the period. On the other hand, the rapid pace of technical change may have increased the extent to which they acted as constraints on the freedom of employers to adapt their methods of working. The third, most usual mode of action was application of leverage by the threat of strikes or other types of collective action by the labour-force of a factory, firm, or industry.

In the period from 1933 to 1969 the number of working-days lost per year varied quite a lot from year to year, but was always below, and normally very substantially below, ten million. This was a level that had quite often been exceeded, sometimes substantially, in the 1920s and before the First World War, and which was again exceeded in 1970, 71, 72, and 1974. These statistics understate the scale of disruption because they do not include the consequential suspension of other jobs outside the factory in which the strike occurred, and this may be a factor of greater relative importance in more recent times. On the other hand, the later figures do relate to a larger total labour-force.

However, strikes, like earthquakes and wars, are essentially abnormal events reflecting collision and inconsistent movements of components rather than the extent of the underlying changes that may be occurring. The underlying shift in the relative power of labour and captial is not one on which simple direct evidence exists. The events of actual strikes do no more than provide us, and potential combatants, with evidence of the effectiveness of weaponry, and the incidence of strikes tells us no more about industrial relations than that of wars tells us about the importance of relative military strength in the evolution of international relations.

In the short and medium term the strength of the incumbent labour-force is that its absence from work causes the employer a loss that is very much bigger than its positive contribution when in work. This would always be the case because of the natural difficulty and expense of retaining replacement labour, but was enhanced by the widespread acceptance of the right to prevent 'black-legging' and of the right to intervene in the conduct of a company's general business by the blacking of supplies to it and of its products (such intervention often at no cost to those imposing it) — a category of action visibly extended by the miners in their disruption of power station operations in 1972 and 1974. Behind the undoubted increase in the coercive power of organized labour lay different types of development. The resources available to the State declined with the reduction in size of the Army; and governments of both parties after 1950 lacked the resolution demonstrated by the Attlee government when it put troops into the docks in 1948 and 1949. Thus employers had to accept that even where industrial action endangered the public interest, and more widely where it led to actions that were, strictly, illegal, they could not depend on having their rights enforced. Apart from these prominent, but extreme and perhaps relatively rare, cases, the basic economic vulnerability of many businesses had been increased by changes in the nature of technology: the greater importance of fixed capital and of indirect labour increased the element of fixed cost that would still have to be incurred even in the absence of a large part of the labour-force; the increased integration of productive processes made the absence of one part of the labour-force have a disproportionately damaging effect; and, in the case of firms with the apparent advantage of being monopolistic suppliers of distinct branded products, interruption of supply damaged the goodwill of distributors and customers.

It was often said that the ability of the labour-force to strike was enhanced by, in comparison with former times, the relative generosity of social security payments for families and the ability to obtain refunds of income tax. However, strikes were not notably long by international standards and strikers did not show the extra stamina that might have been expected from their higher real incomes. The fact that with hire-purchase payments and mortgages their members' short-term commitments had fully kept pace with their incomes was perhaps the most vulnerable aspect of the unions' position. They did nothing to remedy this, and strike funds were, in real terms, surprisingly small. But this perhaps was a reflection of unions' confidence in their ability to avoid strikes because of the visible weakness of employers.

As has been emphasized earlier, the nature of work changed to reduce the number of jobs in which something objectively definable was continually delivered by the employee. Consequently, in many more cases than formerly employees could press their case without striking by witholding willing and intelligent co-operation.

In such cases employers, because of their concern to regain co-operation, were likely to be very hesitant to incur the opprobium of 'locking-out' by suspending employees, although their net productivity might have fallen far below the wage they continued to receive.

It might be thought that the growing size of firms would have increased the power of employers to resist. In one way it clearly did. The large firm, especially one already organized on a multi-national basis, could react to trouble by shifting some of its activity overseas and, in the last resort, closing down its U.K. operations. However, the latter extreme course, which would involve abandoning the capital already sunk in the U.K. branch, limited rather than eliminated the unions bargaining power. Apart from this, the increased size of firms probably increased the power of labour. The increased remoteness of ultimate management and control made it easier for the organizers of labour to build up a 'we/they' attitude. In so far as firms had exploited economies that required integration of their various operations they provided more visible targets for supplementary coercive action. Finally the more the increase in the size of the firm had brought them greater control of their market, the harder it was for them to plead that they were limited by a competitive market in the costs they could incur.

The discussion above has followed economic practice in characterizing the changes described as having increased the monopoly power of unions — but this simple description requires qualification. Even if at heart they are ruthless maximizers, monopolists are faced by lack of knowledge of the full extent of their power and of the full consequences of their actions; they may therefore be cautious of taking full advantage of the increased power that changed circumstances have given them. But in any case unions could not be ruthless profit-maximizers: for exercise of their full potential coercive power required mobilization of the enthusiasm of their members and the neutrality if not co-operation of some non-members — both of which depended on a view of the rightness of their cause. Unions were, moreover, large and remote. The main consequence of this was a widespread devolution of effective power to shop-stewards. Sometimes local agreements with individual managements left national agreements of little consequence.

The picture then is not one of very abrupt change. It is much more one of unions exploring the extent of their power cautiously, at least as they saw it; knowing that in many cases there must be some limit to the extent to which they could push up the price of their labour without pushing some small firms into bankruptcy, and multi-nationals to shift the balance of their operations; knowing, too, that the concern of their members with the steadiness of their pay-packets limited their capacity for mobilization. But the existence of these restraints did not guarantee stability. The limits to which the profits of a firm could be squeezed were not clearly perceptible, and there was no means of telling exactly when they had been overshot. And though many unions might agree that the rewards their labour would receive in a competitive market were too low there was no consensus about what they were entitled to. With the persistence of inflation and the slow growth of disposable income, it was possible for there to be cumulatively a great pressure forward, itself creating inflation, without any part of the labour-force thinking that it was doing any more than trying to maintain a position, the right to which it considered that it had previously established. The effect of union power on the average level of wages and hence on inflation, and, via restrictive practices, on investment is discussed elsewhere; its effect on relative wages is discussed in the next section.

Collective agreements themselves involve the establishment of grades, and in some cases the desire of unions to protect their position involves further standardization. Thus, for example, there was no question of older workers being paid less; and the wage rates of juveniles were kept high to prevent their becoming cheap substitutes for adult labour. The natural consequence of standardization was that the value to the employer of many employees (actual and potential) did not match the grades, and such employees were not engaged or tended to become redundant. This is not to blame all such redundancy on grading enforced by unions. Standardization was also a consequence of the bureaucratic requirements of large firms. And the technical change which made it infeasible to match pay with individual output could also make it a sensible policy to play safe by offering high wages and choosing from the excess of applicants only those whose capabilities clearly exceeded requirements.

Such policies by firms and unions tended to separate the labour market into two parts: the one comprising the regular employees of large firms, fitting a pattern of grades determined by collective agreement (and possibly by the firms' procedures); the other a collection of residual categories. This latter included: executives who had lost their place and were too old, or 'too qualified', to be fitted into bureaucratic pyramids; pensioners from the police or the services; the elderly chosen for premature retirement under redundancy schemes; women wanting to work limited hours; and a large supply of other part-time labour, including individuals seeking second employment.

The course of diffrent types of earnings

Table 6.3 Distribution of earnings of male manual workers

	1938	1960	1968	1974	1977
Median Earnings £ (weekly)	3·4	14·2	22·4	41·8	68·2
Lowest Decile as percentage of Median	67·7	70·6	67·3	68·6	70·6
Lower Quartile as percentage of Median	82·1	82·6	81·0	82·2	83·1
Upper Quartile as percentage of Median	118·5	121·7	122·3	121·0	120·3
Highest Decile as percentage of Median	139·9	145·2	147·8	144·1	144·4

Note: Lowest decile means earnings of the worker 10 per cent of the way up the list from the bottom. Lowest quartile means earnings of the worker 25 per cent of the way up the list. Median means earnings half way up list.

Amongst male manual workers the range of incomes remained wide. In 1977 as many workers earned under £68.20 as earned more than that amount. 10 per cent of workers (the lowest decile) received less than 70 per cent of this median and 25 per cent (the lowest quartile) receive less than 83 per cent, while at the other extreme 10 per cent received more than 140 per cent. As Table 6.3 shows, these proportions were not very different from those in 1960 and 1938 (or indeed from those shown in fragmentary evidence for 1886) — somewhat difficult to reconcile with the impression sometimes given of a continual narrowing of differentials. In fact there was a falling of the ratio between the wages of a skilled fitter and an engineering labourer from about 140 per cent in 1939 to 125 per cent in 1951, but the next 16 years saw the widening of the gap to 140 per cent in 1967, from which there was a narrowing. But the differentials shown in Table 6.3 are probably mainly the consequence of differences between industries. There were important differences between occupations requiring men in their prime to work intensively, and where overtime working and premium working were common, and others where work was less demanding and hours more limited. To some extent there was a systematic shift of labour in its working life from the one to the other, and an increased proportion of employment was in these latter occupations.

Statistical comparisons of comparable jobs in intensively and lightly unionized industries suggest that in the 1970s collective bargaining might cause earnings to be 20 per cent higher than they would otherwise have been; a similar study for the early sixties suggested a differential of perhaps 10 per cent. (Both estimates are very tentative.) There are clear cases where union-based monopolies caused wages to be very much higher than they would have been if there had been a free inflow from similar jobs. The disputes in the 1970s about what was 'dockers' work' in neighbouring parts of the cargo-handling trade were related to such a differential. More notable for the very high levels of earnings were certain jobs on national newspapers. But such examples, which attracted attention, can be seen from the detailed surveys of earnings to have been very exceptional.

Between 1938 and 1948 the average hourly earnings of women manual workers in all industries rose from 51·6 per cent to 60·6 per cent of the male average. Thereafter there was a decline back to 59·4 per cent of the male average in 1969. It is unlikely that this trend was the consequence of an increase in differential in favour of men within individual trades. It is much more likely to have been caused by the more rapid growth of earnings in trades dominated by men than those where women were of greater importance. However, although to some extent this was a matter of chance (for example, the concentration of women in trades like textiles and clothing, subject to extreme pressures of foreign competition) it may also reflect simple supply and demand factors, that is, the increasing supply of female labour for those trades. Another differential to be noted is that between young and adult workers. Young male earnings increased from 39·0 per cent of the adult male level in 1938 to 45·0 per cent in 1948 and had increased again to 51·6 per cent by 1968. By contrast, the earnings of young women increased from 28·7 per cent of the adult male level in 1938 to 39·5 per cent in 1948 and were still at the same level in 1968.

Because there was less official concern for the welfare of non-manual labour, information about its earnings is much slighter than for manual labour. Between 1938 and 1955 the real earnings of non-manual labour rose slowly, and in some individual cases may have declined. Reported salaries fell, as a percentage of manual earnings, from 136 per cent in 1938 to 123 per cent in 1955.

This could be explained as a lack of bargaining power, but it is better to explain it as a lack of organization to press for frequent adjustment of salaries and, possibly, a willingness to accept the 1940s as a period of prolonged abnormality. In the later 1950s the differential increased and reached 128 per cent in 1969 — the consequence of unionization and more militancy in some cases, and, conceivably, also an active demand for certain types of non-manual skill. Finally in the 1970s the differential narrowed again to 124 per cent as a consequence of incomes policies.

The non-manual group included a wide variety of jobs from junior clerks to senior professional men and executives at or near the top of organizational pyramids. Its dispersion of incomes was consequently much wider than the manual group with, in the late 1970s, the earnings of the top 10 per cent at least some three times higher than those of the bottom 10 per cent. The dispersion of these incomes narrowed in the 1970s because of Incomes Policy, and had almost certainly narrowed between 1938 and the 1950s. It is much less clear what happened between 1950 and 1970. It must, of course, be remembered that in addition to any narrowing of differentials in terms of earnings, the much higher levels of direct taxation had a general tendency to narrow differentials in net take-home pay — in some phases very severely.

How far were changes (and absence of changes) in the pattern of differentials the consequence of economic factors? How far, on the other hand, were the changes caused by the increasing dominance of systems of valuation of work that had no rationale in simple market factors of supply and demand. Ostensibly non-economic factors were of increasing importance. They operated within large unions in so far as there was a tendency to assimilate individual cases to general categories. Quite separately, they originated within organizations where, as in the Army, the assessment of the appropriate differentials between ranks is more a sociological than an economic phenomenon — a characteristic common to many public bodies and also to many large companies. But they also derived from the practice of external adjudication (as distinct from arbitration) by Courts of Inquiry set up to deal with serious industrial disputes. Such a Court declared in 1955:

Having willed the ends, the Nation must will the means. This implies that the employees of such a national service should receive a fair and adequate wage, and that, in broad terms, the railwayman should be in no worse case than his colleagues in comparable industry.

By contrast with national incomes policies, which had a distinct tendency to narrow differentials, most of these factors tended to conserve established differentials.

However, the system with relatively rigid differentials related to organizational status was not completely dominant. There were many parts of the economy in which institutional influences were quite unimportant. Particularly in the period of full employment, all parts of the economy were subject to market influence.

At the top of the scale, the incomes of leading musicians and entertainers were increased by the effect of television and the improvement of sound recording in increasing the size of their audiences — an effect magnified still further by air travel which enabled stars to perform in widely distributed locations offering the highest fees without having either to reduce the number of their performances or to sacrifice their freedom to live where conditions most attracted them. Less spectacularly, the salaries of those connected with computer programming reflected a newly developed demand for a relatively scarce natural ability. The salaries of secretaries, on the whole, depended on their scarcity in the market rather than effective unionization. As we have seen, between 1951 and 1967 there was a widening of the gap between the wages of skilled engineers and unskilled labourers. On the other hand, the wages in many sectors providing suitable employment for women or the elderly were relatively low, at least until the operation of the Equal Pay Act 1968, because of the growth in the supply of these kinds of labour.

But over a wide area it is more difficult to discern with confidence whether changes were caused by economic forces. The long-term compression and even reversal of differentials, particularly those between manual and non-manual occupations, was often seen by those adversely affected as a disturbance of the natural order and a consequence of the improper use of monopoly power. That there were some, possibly many, cases of exploitative monopoly is not disputed; but the general change observed would not have surprised Adam Smith. Prima facie the two most important changes affecting supply and demand in the labour market were the enormous increase in the supply of labour that had received secondary and higher education, and the general rise in real incomes. The first of these factors, if other things had been equal, might have been expected to reduce, or even eliminate, the premiums obtainable for having been educated. The effect of the second might have been expected to be a rise in the relative premiums required to persuade people who might otherwise have done ordinary jobs to take on those that were dangerous, dirty, in some other way onerous, or merely inconvenient. That, for a time, the compression ceased in the late fifties and sixties may have been either because wartime saw an over-narrowing or because, for a time, the expansion of certain types of employment made some skills (including the general skills inculcated by higher education) scarce again. Ostensibly the subsequent narrowing was entirely due to the externally imposed constraints of incomes policies; but in their absence it is uncertain whether the constant differentials of the 1960s would have been maintained.

7 Income wealth and their distribution

Average income

By deducting capital consumption, the proportion of Gross National Product that has to be devoted to making good the deterioration and obsolescence of the capital stock, we obtain net national product or national income. This, expressed in constant (1970) pounds per head of population, increased from £395 in 1937 to £446 in 1948 (1·1 per cent p.a) to £540 in 1958 (1·9 per cent p.a.) to £693 in 1968 (2·5 per cent p.a.) to £778 in 1974 (2·0 per cent p.a.). This overall increase fell short of the aspirations of R. A. Butler, who as Chancellor in 1952 hoped to double the standard of living in the next twenty years, but was substantial by comparison with any earlier period (for example, 1·5 per cent in the period 1924–37).

The growth of *per capita* employment income (that is, wages and salaries) was distinctly faster than the growth of the average of all incomes because of the increasing share of labour in the national income. Between 1938 and 1948 labour's share rose from 63 per cent to 70 per cent. For the next twenty years its share was effectively approximately constant, because although it showed a further increase to 74 per cent, there was concurrently a fall of about the same size in the proportion accruing to the 'self-employed' as a consequence of the decline in very small businesses, most of whose income should be seen as a labour payment. Then, in the late sixties and early seventies, there was a further sharp shift until, in 1975, 82 per cent of national income accrued to employed labour without any further fall in the share of the self-employed. If the rate of profit on capital had remained constant during this period, the increasing ratio of capital to output would have required the percentage share of labour in output to fall. That labour's share actually rose, and rose markedly, is the counterpart of the fall of profits to a very low level indeed.

If therefore we consider *employment* income per head of the population, we see a growth between 1937 and 1948 of 2·0 per cent per annum (higher than between 1924 and 1937 when it was 1·5 per cent) and between 1948 and 1974 of 2·6 per cent (within the latter period the cumulative growth was only a little short of a doubling). Within this period there was an acceleration from 2·2 per cent in 1948–58, to 2·7 per cent in 1958–68, and 3·1 per cent in 1968–74.

Table 7.1 Rate of growth (per cent per annum) of income per head

	1924–37	37–48	48–58	58–68	68–74
All income per head of population	1·5	1·1	1·9	2·5	2·0
Employment income per head of population	1·5	2·0	2·2	2·7	3·1
Employment income per head of employed population	0·7	1·8	2·1	3·0	3·8
Personal disposable income per head of population	n.a.	0·0	2·2	2·5	3·2

Up to about 1960 employment income per head of the population was growing more quickly than income per employed person, after the early sixties more slowly. This is the counterpart of the fact that up to 1960 the proportion of the population employed was increasing, but that it declined thereafter. This growth in the ratio of income-earners to population was an important element in the growth of real income per head between the Wars, made a noticeable contribution between 1937 and 1948, but only a slight contribution to the growth of the next ten years.

For two reasons the share of profits in G.N.P. was not the same as the share of 'unearned income' in the income actually received by persons. First, interest on the public debt is treated as a 'transfer'. To the extent that it is paid out of taxation on employment incomes, it may therefore understate the relative importance of 'unearned income': interest on the public debt increased in relative importance between 1938 and 1948, but was subsequently reduced because of the effect of inflation. Second, and working in the opposite direction, not all the profits of companies were distributed to their individual shareholders; the proportion retained increased until the mid-fifties, fell for the next decade, and then generally increased because of the effect of dividend control. Such 'unearned' incomes halved in relative importance (from about 20 per cent to about 10 per cent of personal incomes) between 1938 and 1948, and had almost halved again by 1975 (to 5·5 per cent). Moreover, in 1975 almost half of dividends accrued to insurance and pension funds, compared with about an eighth in 1951, implying a much wider, though by no means even, scattering. The proportionate importance of rent and dividends in incomes directly received in 1975 was no more than a sixth of what it had been in 1938. (This statistic may be held to understate the importance of such income because it excludes payments of interest from one part of the personal sector to another which if included would have doubled the 1975 proportion — though still leaving it only a third of 1938.)

A question that arises is how the statistical picture which actually shows as high growth of income per head in 1961–74, as in 1948–61, is to be reconciled with the evident contentment of the electorate in responding to the slogan 'You've never had it so good' in 1959 and the persistent grumbles about incomes in the subsequent period. We have to be cautious in the weight we attach to individual impressions on this sort of matter. This is particularly true of the period of the seventies when life became a continuous series of wage-claims and almost everybody acquired a motive for publicly bewailing the pressures on their living standards. The process of inflation itself obscured trends because of its asymmetry: increases in prices occurred more or less continuously, increases in wage rates only occasionally, so that even if the latter kept fully in step with prices, the impression of individuals was that, for most of the time, their real incomes were declining. Furthermore, experience was measured against expectations, but expectations were related not only to politicians' promises but also to hopes of individual advancement attached either to the achievement of educational qualifications or to occupations where an increase in salary was expected with time. It is quite possible that the growing importance of employment in the professions, and in organizations where there were increments for age and experience, could have created a situation in which a continual rise in average income would have been necessary just to match these individual expectations. The individuals concerned did not see their own incomes as rising because they took no account of the benefit in which they had participated of there being more relatively highly paid jobs than in previous years. Similarly, when employed on incremental scales they naturally incorporated those in their expectations of the job they held: again taking no account of the likelihood that simple satisfaction of these expectations would require an increase in average incomes.

The statistics we are examining are of income per head of the *population*. As explained above, a part of the increase came from an increase in the proportion of the population of working age who were employed. The increase in the post-war period was entirely due to the employment of married women. By no means the whole, and perhaps not even most, of the incomes brought into existence were regarded by their recipients as a net gain: as well as the expenses of travelling to work, the need to economize on time spent on household tasks involved extra outlays, on 'convenience foods', replacing instead of mending clothes, and perhaps the employment of paid domestic service. Distance from home to work, and, therefore, expenses in travelling to work became greater for most employees, and while some of the increase was associated with an improvement in living conditions, a great deal was associated with the increased scale of factories and businesses, and would more properly be regarded as an expense of production to be deducted from G.D.P.

Probably the most important factor that disguised the extent of the rise in real incomes, was the increase from about 1960 of the proportionate importance of government expenditure and the taxation needed to finance it. This increase was concentrated on direct rather than indirect taxation and on personal rather than corporate taxation. Although taxation financed expenditures that were of public benefit, or grants to the needy that the community would need to make in some way or other, the expenditures were not generally accepted as being a 'social wage', either because of scepticism about the management of the expenditure or because though individuals approved of the expenditures they did not automatically recognize any consequent obligation to finance their share.

A different qualification of the statistical picture is also needed.

Measures of price are very imperfect at making allowance for the changing quality of goods, particularly new goods. The fifties saw the introduction of goods of great novelty and utility to a wide range of consumers, black-and-white television, synthetic fibres in textiles, and plastics in a great variety of uses at prices very much less than many consumers would have willingly paid for them. Consumer innovation did not stop in 1959, but it is difficult to see innovations of the same value in the subsequent period.

Moreover, the course of economic change after 1959 brought more disruption for individuals. Consumers had to accept standardization by producers of goods, and curtailment of services; and the labour-force had to accept the dislocation of redundancy. On the other hand, in listing factors qualifying the simple statistical measure of improvement in real income we should not ignore the decline in the hours of work (at least for the male population) and generally a substantial improvement in working conditions. The number of deaths from industrial injuries declined (though it remained shockingly high and some new causes of mortality were revealed); in many places mechanization removed much of the physical onerousness of work; while the extensive rebuilding of offices improved the working conditions of non-manual workers. Against this are more imponderable matters — whether in some cases the pace and stress of work increased; and whether these detriments themselves were not entirely matters of objective physiology but were aggravated by the scale and remoteness of large organizations.

From the mid-sixties there was an increasingly wide consciousness of the disadvantages of economic growth which are not accounted for adequately, or even included, in Gross Domestic Product. The limited supply of land and its associated amenities were particularly apparent in a relatively small country as the number of households increased and as the modernization of industry required increasingly spacious layouts. As mobility and leisure time increased, remote places became less remote and sometimes became so crowded that the qualities originally enjoyed were destroyed altogether. Another, inevitable, cause of disappointment came from the fact that as everybody got richer and incomes became more equal it was not possible for everybody to enjoy those luxuries previously enjoyed by the rich that depended on service. Some would extend the argument to more subjective matters: the enjoyment that came from the possession of unique objects and pride in above-average performance are not, by their nature, purchaseable by all. On the other hand, since the range of leisure activities was very widely extended and the absolute quality of much performance improved, it is not clear how fundamentally enjoyment was qualified by the inability of everybody to be first.

Growth brought change, and change was often to the disadvantage of individuals, in some cases with no or inadequate compensation: the noise and danger of motor traffic; noise more generally; interference with views; the discordant accumulation of individual building developments. It may be that there were factors that made these problems more acute in the third quarter of the twentieth century: the very completeness of the redevelopment of the centre of towns, and the anarchic individualism of road traffic. But it should be remembered that consciousness of these detriments was itself to some extent a product of a standard of living less concerned with basic necessities; and that their long and loud articulation was part of the political process of obtaining redress and protection not previously available to the same extent.

Some detriments of industrialization which had been common and increasing for a hundred years yielded to legislation: visible smoke and, less completely, river pollution. New problems emerged, particularly those associated with the development of new chemical processes. And beyond the dangers actually identified there was increasing worry that other, more gradually working, effects had still to be perceived. This was part of a more general intellectual concern with the future which included a consciousness of the limits of natural resources that had perhaps not been as widespread since the opening-up a hundred years before of the non-European continents.

The distribution of income

Table 7.2 is, at first sight, in conflict with what has been said about the declining importance of unearned income from dividends and

Table 7.2 Percentage distribution of income before and after tax

| | Before Tax | | | After Tax | | |
	1938–39	1949–50	1974–75	1938–39	1949–50	1974–75
Top 1%	17·1	10·6	5·9	11·7	5·8	3·8
next 2–5%	14·4	12·5	9·9	13·6	10·9	9·1
6–10%	9·0	9·0	9·0	9·3	9·0	8·8
11–20%	11·9	13·2	14·6	12·7	13·7	14·7
21–30%	8·8	10·6	12·3	9·6	11·1	12·6
31–70%	24·9	30·3	35·0	27·7	33·5	36·2
71–100%	13·8	13·8	13·3	15·4	15·9	14·8

Source: Royal Commission on Distribution of Income and Wealth (I & W) Report 5 Tables D5 and D7 (Cmnd 6999)

the narrowing differential between manual and non-manual earnings. Apart from the fall in the share of the top five per cent of incomes, there seems to have been little change in the relative shares of the remainder of the population, except that the share of the bottom thirty per cent rose distinctly less than that of the middle sixty per cent. The latter point can probably be entirely explained by the increase in the relative number of retired people in the population. Since most pensioners had lower incomes than those who were employed, an increase in their numbers would naturally increase the relative number of low income households, even though the incomes of pensioners as individuals had generally improved relative to the rest of the population. (A separate, more technical, point is that the statistics relate to 'tax-units' and not individuals. Because of the increase in the number of pensioners, and for other reasons, there was an increase in the relative number of tax-units with a small number of persons. Consequently what is shown in the table as the bottom thirty per cent of units contained a smaller proportion of the total population in 1974/5 than it had in 1938/9 or 1949/50.)

At the other end of the table, better-paid jobs may not have been as well paid in relative terms, but there were very many more of them because of the expansion of employment in the professions and because of the growth of hierarchical organizations. At the very top, the number of income earners with £10,000 + (in 1974–5 pounds) increased by seventy per cent between 1960 and 1974, and a similar effect operated further down the scale in many categories of white-collar employment. A professor in 1975 might compare his income adversely with that of a professor in 1938: what he was less likely to do was to compare the likelihood of his being a professor in 1975 with the likelihood that he would have become one in 1938. In short, the size of prizes offered in life's lottery may have been reduced, but the number was increased. To try to summarize the result as more or less equality is to divert attention from the fact that there were two changes, each important in itself.

Despite the high level of taxation, the effect of income tax made little difference to the shape of the income distribution described above. In 1938/9 only the top five per cent of incomes had a lower proportionate share after than before income tax; in the post-war period this redistributive effect extended to the next five per cent as well — but to a barely perceptible extent. That there was so little effect reflects the basic shape of British direct taxation in the post-war period — a very long range of incomes on which the same full standard rate of tax was paid.

The very high rates of taxation provided incentives for arrangements that were beneficial to individuals but did not constitute the receipt of taxable income, benefits of which no account is taken in the statistics. Although such re-arrangements were most notorious amongst the highest incomes, it should not be assumed that all the highest incomes were understated or that lesser incomes were not understated at all. Tax avoidance may qualify the impression given by the statistics; but it does not reverse it.

High levels of taxation contributed to, though were not the main factor in, the spread of pension funds, because savings accumulated therein and the interest they earned were free of income tax. For most of the period, the membership of pension schemes was much higher amongst salaried staff than amongst manual workers. The existence of these large funds is an important qualification to the increased equality of current earnings — and was reflected in the very different levels of income within the retired class. It could, moreover, be argued that the most usual type of scheme that related pension to salaries immediately before retirement, a stage in life at which they tended to be most unequal, allocated a disproportionate part of the employers' contributions to those whose salaries had increased most during their careers, and was consequently a powerful mechanism making for inequality.

The real benefits accruing to individuals and to classes are affected by relative changes of prices as well as of incomes. Inflation tended to obscure the changes of relative prices that had occurred during the forty years — some of which were very considerable. The most general cause of such changes in relative prices was differences in the extent to which innovation in goods and in processes of production together with economies of scale had offset increases in labour costs. At one extreme are some manufactured goods where there were very large increases in productivity — especially if changes in product quality are allowed for. The cost in shillings of a minute of music recorded on a gramophone record in 1975 was little if any more than in the 1930s, despite its better quality. In other cases, durable goods, clothes and possibly cars, prices were higher, but, allowing for quality improvements, had not increased by as much as the average of prices generally. At the other extreme were pure labour services, like taxis or window-cleaning, where there was little scope for adaptation to save labour and where consequently the rise in prices simply reflected the rise in labour costs. Beyond these cases were a few, for example, road passenger transport, where the change in relative prices caused a loss of demand and a consequent loss of economies of scale, which tended to cause prices to rise even further for a service of worse quality for the customers who remained.

For those whose small incomes confined their expenditure to necessities, the overall trend was probably relatively adverse, since their expenditures on manufactures whose price fell most was proportionately small. Quite how adverse depended on whether labour services (like transport) were an important part of consumption, and this varied considerably between individuals. This group was, on the other hand, a beneficiary of the long favourable movement in terms of trade because of the relatively large part of its income spent on food and, conversely, was hit relatively hard by the relative increase of food prices after 1970. It may be assumed that above these low levels of income the tendency to spend extra income on maufactured goods is greatest, and that it is in these middle ranges that relative gains in real income are most understated by changes in money incomes.

Above this wide band of middling incomes the net balance is more mixed and generalization is less easy. For some households labour services were an important category of expenditure (an important example being private education); in others, consumption was much more of goods and those items whose relative price had fallen. In assessing real benefits we should not be exclusively concerned with the cost of maintaining a particular initial pattern of expenditure; for at high levels of expenditure there was considerable scope for obtaining the same net benefits by adapting the actual pattern of expenditure to newly available possibilities. In particular we should notice that the very many devices and products that reduced the need for domestic labour by housewives also reduced the need for the paid labour of servants. These labour-saving effects were multiplied, since in the households of Edwardian and earlier times, the larger the establishment of servants, the lower had been the proportion of their labours devoted to the service of the families employing them and the higher the proportion to the service of other servants.

The poor

In 1950 Seebohm Rowntree found only 3 per cent of the population of York to be in primary poverty. This can be compared with his previous investigations when he found 6·8 per cent primary poverty in 1936, and 15·5 per cent in 1899. By a less harsh standard, the scale used in 1953/4 for determining the grant of National Assistance, 4·8 per cent of the whole country were in poverty in 1953/4, and poverty had virtually vanished by 1973. Since, however, the criterion of poverty used for administration was raised by 50 per cent in real terms between 1953 and 1973, 2·3 per cent of the population were still eligible for benefit in 1973.

The causes of poverty changed, with unemployment being a very much less important factor. The poor were the elderly, single women with dependent children, and low-paid men with large families. As previously, sharp variations in relative financial comfort could occur within a working life: teenagers with high wages relative to needs became 'young marrieds' paying high rents while waiting for a place on the housing list, and had expenses of equipping a house and providing for children; a position eased by a wife's earnings, eased further when children ceased to be dependent, worsened by retirement.

By an absolute standard there was a considerable amelioration of the position of the poor, but a consciousness of inequalities remained. No doubt this was in part explicable as a change in attitudes and standards produced by greater general knowledge about how other classes lived, but it was also related to several objective factors.

The greatest improvement in real incomes accrued to the broad mass of the working class and the lower middle classes who spent most on manufactured goods, that is, to the class most likely to be in contact with, indeed intermingled with, many of the poor. This made contrasting standards of living very obvious, but it also had a second more direct effect. The favourable change of prices depended on economies of scale, which in turn depended on a degree of standardization of goods. Manufacturers and retailers looking for levels of quality on which to standardize naturally focused on families with average purchasing power, with the result that there was a decline in the availability of plainer goods, and indeed a continuous 'trading up' as the period progressed. There was nothing new in the more prosperous having better clothes and better food; what was new was that they got them at bargain prices at Marks & Spencer. A phenomenon with a similar economic cause, but aggravated by the rise in labour costs, was the decline in public transport: those too poor to own cars were the most severely affected — a condition aggravated where public housing redevelopment had increased travelling distances. Poverty was often aggravated by lack of efficient household management. Education might have improved, but the variety of goods was wider and, often, their qualities more difficult to appraise. Other facets of life, obtaining houses, obtaining benefits, also became more complicated for those who had had a poor education.

For observers in the 1970s, the problem of poverty often seemed

Table 7.3 Total stock of houses in U.K.

	1938	1950	1960	1970	1974
Value of Gross Stock at 1970 Prices (£ thousand millions)	28·1	30·8	38·3	51·4	57·8
Number in thousands					
Owner Occupied:		4100	6967	9567	10536
Public Rented:		2500	4400	5848	6228
Private Rented:		6200	4306	3768	3331
		13900	16600	19183	20095

to be closely related to the housing problem. As a percentage of G.D.P. the expenditure on housing was high over the period as a whole. By international standards, Britain began and finished the period with one of the best housing stocks relative to population. What then was the housing problem?

Rent control imposed during the First World War, subsequently relaxed, and then re-imposed, and though modified during the 1950s against a background of building costs which rose much more than average prices, killed the attractiveness of building houses for rent — which was, until 1914, a popular investment with small and middling savers. The stock of such houses gradually decreased, primarily through sales to owner occupiers — but also through deterioration accelerated by inadequate repair. Though incomes rose, the ratio of average income to new house prices rose little because of increased land prices and, particularly, because of the higher than average rise in building costs. Together with the rise in interest rates on mortgages, this increased the money outlay required to buy a house relative to average income and limited the extent to which former renters could become owner-occupiers.

The stock of second-hand houses, whether for rent or owner occupation, was reduced by indiscriminate clearances by municipal authorities, whose natural inclination to the spectacular and the administratively simple was reinforced, until the late sixties, by the system of central government subsidies. The stock was further diminished by extensive rebuilding of city centres to provide retailers with larger floor areas, and to accommodate the increasing number of office workers. Competition for the remaining houses was increased by a reversal of the process by which, during the previous century, the better-off had been moving further and further from city centres, leaving their cast-off housing to augment the stock available to those less well-off. In the sixties the elimination of coal smoke by the Clean Air Act, the end of coal gas production and of steam locomotion, made living in the central areas attractive to the better-off, who were willing to pay a premium to avoid commuting.

Several factors diminished the efficiency with which the housing stock was used. For the whole period after the War, security of tenure combined with rent control and the high taxation of 'unearned' incomes made unfurnished property an unattractive asset for landlords, who often held properties empty or under-occupied until they could be sold. For most of the period the alternative was furnished letting, where there was no security of tenure and where high rents were the consequence of the overspill of demand from the rest of the market. After security of tenure was given in 1974 to furnished tenants, much of this supply was withdrawn. At the same time houses for owner-occupation were attractive as assets; they yielded benefits to their owners which were not taxed, and experience suggested their value kept pace with inflation. Consequently there was probably much more demand for, and under-use of, housing than there would have been if there had been no inflation and if the ownership of housing had been subject to a higher level of taxation. Although municipal housing could be initially allocated on the basis of relative need, it would have been unacceptable to re-allocate it continually. As time went by, older tenants acquired vested interests in their preferential position and the stock had a tendency to become increasingly under-used and its relatively low rents were paid by tenants who, on average, had distinctly higher incomes than those who had to pay high rents for the limited stock of expensive private accommodation.

Housing was important in aggravating poverty not only because the expenditure on rents in the remaining private market constituted a large proportion of the income of poor people, but also because individual circumstances varied so widely. The variation was partly geographical, for the factors above operated much more powerfully in London and other cities than elsewhere. It was also individual; some people who had a low income nevertheless owned their own houses; and others enjoyed the relative insulation of protected tenancies. This variation of condition among people who otherwise had the same income contributed to the difficulty of administering poverty relief.

The distribution of wealth

Several processes operated in the growth and distribution of personal wealth.

Simple accumulation by saving and decumulation by dissaving.

The level of personal saving was temporarily very low in the post-war period — presumably because of the spending of savings made in wartime in replenishing stocks of consumer goods and perhaps also because of the stagnant real incomes of many salary earners. From that time the proportion of personal income saved rose from 1·4 per cent in 1950 to 12·7 per cent in 1974. This includes the very large accumulation of securities and property by pension funds and insurance companies which was indirectly 'accumulation by persons', for it almost entirely comprised savings by individuals or by employers on their behalf.

The 12·7 per cent was the resultant of some individuals saving and others dissaving. We have no estimates, but the extent of dissaving was probably quite large. The fact that land and property became more widely owned with the growth of owner-occupation had its counterpart in the sales of property and building plots by other persons. And there was a fairly continual and very large net selling of company securities by 'persons' to institutions. It must be the case that many of the more wealthy were, on balance, disposing of assets: partly because the accrual of 'capital gains' in money terms encouraged them to spend more than their income; partly to finance 'capital taxation'. Under the system that operated until replaced by Capital Transfer Tax in 1974, Estate Duty was notoriously avoided, but nevertheless during the years 1939–74 it and other taxes on capital averaged just under 1 per cent of G.N.P. per annum; accumulated over the 35 years it constituted a very substantial subtraction from the wealth of the families paying it.

The effect of inflation on the real values of debts.

In so far as the debtors were persons or companies, the process led to a transfer of wealth within the wealth-owning class. The outstanding example was the effect of inflation on building society mortgages for house purchase: here the gain was widely diffused amongst the millions who financed the purchase of their houses by borrowing at the expense of millions of depositors. Where public bodies were indebted to persons or to institutions holding their savings, the gain was diffused over the whole tax-paying population. Within the class of wealth-owners, the effect of inflation was probably very regressive, since the largest proportionate holders of assets, the repayment value of which was fixed in money terms, tended to be those with least wealth. This was also probably true of the net effect of building societies, since some of the lending was by people with very much lower incomes that those who borrowed.

Valuation of real assets

Experience of inflation made real assets attractive and, from the mid-fifties, this was reflected in an increase in the ratio between their price and the income they yielded. However, in the case of industrial shares this was only an improvement relative to bonds, for over the whole period the rise in share prices did not match the rise in prices of goods.

Land values.

In the twenty years from the early fifties land values rose twentyfold or more in most parts of the country, increasing the wealth in money terms both of owner-occupiers and landowners. Rents rose rapidly too — though by smaller proportions — reflecting the fact that property was coming to be valued on a 'premium' basis, because it was thought to constitute a good hedge against inflation.

There were different factors operating in the growth in value of land. Agricultural land belatedly followed the prosperity of farming when, after 1958, the protection of tenancies was modified to allow farm rents to be revised to follow the levels established in the open market for new tenancies. The valuation of agricultural land was also affected by its favourable treatment for Estate Duty. The increase in the price of suburban housing land was primarily caused by administrative restriction of its supply. The Town and Country Planning Act of 1947 reinforced powers designed to prevent haphazard and scattered development such as had occurred in the inter-war period and to establish and protect green-belts to provide amenity for towns. However administered the purposes of the Act would have reduced the supply of building land and tended to increase some land values. However, the actual size of the gap that did emerge (building land had become worth ten times as much as agricultural land in the early sixties and twenty times as much in the early seventies, although agricultural land itself had risen considerably in value) reflected an administrative policy that very severely restricted the supply of land for development.

The rise in value of land in the centre of towns reflected natural scarcity in the face of growing demand. The growth of towns tended to confer a premium on sites nearer their centres. And the demand for central sites was also increased by the increasing proportion of employment both in public administration and in the central management of large companies — activities for which central siting was, or was thought to be, convenient. The operation of these factors was magnified by the operation of restrictions under both Planning and Distribution of Industry legislation — perhaps the most notorious example being the effect on office rents of George Brown's restrictions of London office building in 1964. The 1947 Act had provisions that would effectively have taxed at 100 per cent the gains arising for the change in the use of land, though not the increasing rents arising from continuation of the same usage. Such an extreme provision would, unless accompanied by compulsory development, have removed all incentive to change use, and was repealed in 1951. Between 1951 and 1972, no special fiscal measures were taken to tax development gains or the general rise in rental incomes. A tax was introduced in 1972 to tax all gains that resulted from redevelopment; and the Community Land Act of 1976 attempted, by a system of compulsory purchase at pre-development value, to appropriate 100 per cent of gains from change of use.

Table 7.4 Distribution of wealth (percentages of total)

	1911-13	1936-38	1954	1960	1960	1973
Top 1%	69	56	43	42	38·2	27·6
2-5%	18	23	28	33	26·1	23·7
6-10%	5	9	8	8	12·4	15·9
11-20%	—	—	—	—	13·1	19·2
bottom 90%	8	12	21	17	23·3	32·8
bottom 80%					10·2	13·6

Individually a few very large fortunes were made very rapidly during the period by 'smart dealing' — by buying undervalued shares, by taking-over under-valued companies, by borrowing money to buy real assets — and these received publicity, and excited much indignation. But, whatever the proper moral judgement on such transactions, it should be noted that the gains of these individuals were at the expense of other slower-moving or less perceptive wealth-owners, not at the expense of labour.

Except for a few years in the late fifties, when asset prices rose very rapidly as a reaction to their stagnation in the previous decade, the position of wealth-owners as a whole was eroded by inflation, the failure of share values to keep up with the price index, and by the steady drain of capital taxes. Only in so far as some wealth-owners were adding to their assets by saving out of their own incomes (or in pension schemes) was this erosion offset.

Although the share of wealth of the most wealthy one per cent of the population fell steadily and considerably while that of the least wealthy ninety per cent grew markedly, the wealth of the groups immediately below the top one per cent increased over the period as a whole. It has sometimes been suggested that this was a reflection not of fundamental change but of the rich redistributing their wealth among their families. This seems very unlikely. Even when divided, the fortunes of very rich families would still leave them within the top 1 per cent, and the scope for such families finding many poor relations in an age of small families was limited. It seems much more likely that the growth in the wealth of the second to twentieth percentiles was due primarily to accumulation within their own lifetimes. In 1975 membership of the top five per cent of wealth-owners required assets of only £18,000, a level easily reached by a lifetime's accumulation without exceptional thrift, in an age when house prices had increased twenty or more times.

8 The managed economy 1939–67

In 1939 the role of the State in the economy was already very different from what it had been in the nineteenth century. The growth of its involvement in social security and education had required an increase in its expenditure in relation to G.D.P. It had intervened to assist the rationalization of specific industries and, more generally, by introducing the Tariff in 1932. It had also increased its involvement in what would subsequently be called the macro-economic management of the economy, through more frequent consultation with the Bank of England, which continued formally to be responsible for monetary policy and the management of the foreign exchanges.

Many thought that the State might play a larger and more detailed part by 'planning' the economy. 'Planning' has now, and did have, two meanings. On the one hand, it might refer to a single grand design: the drawing-up of a list of social priorities to be enforced by nationalization, and by the fiscal and other coercive apparatus of the State — a collectivist socialist view. On the other, it might refer to the role of the State in co-ordinating the economy to avoid the wastes, particularly of unemployment, but also of the surpluses from overproduction that seemed to result from the free operation of the market. Though the belief in the possible gains from this sort of 'staff-work' was widespread amongst socialists, impressed by the achievements claimed for the Plan in the U.S.S.R., it was not confined to them. There was a disposition amongst some non-socialists to accept a managerial philosophy that, in the State as well as in individual business, wastes could be avoided by some systematic organization.

The War itself involved fairly thoroughgoing planning in both senses, that is, enforcement of priorities and detailed co-ordinating staff-work. After the War the apparatus of planning and control was not abandoned as precipitately as it had been after the First

War — but it was gradually, and eventually almost completely, dismantled. This did not leave the situation as it had been in 1939.

The War caused a 'stretching' of what had been accepted as the limits of 'fiscal capacity'. And, even when the bulk of the economic apparatus of wartime control had been dismantled, government retained, and was assumed by most of the population to have, a degree of responsibility for the overall management of the economy that it had not been thought to have before or been thought capable of exercising. To some extent this was a consequence of more or less explicit promises made in the War, but it was also due to a general acceptance that wartime administration had been effective.

Governments in the 1950s were able to satisfy the public requirement that they be in control of the economy without being involved in detailed economic management by their adherence to the fiscal policies of the Keynesian revolution. Certainly, though buffeted by continual balance-of-payments crises, the country for twenty years enjoyed unprecedentedly low unemployment and an unprecedentedly high growth of real incomes, marred only by the reappearance of unemployment in some regions.

Nevertheless, as the period developed there was increasing dissatisfaction with the management of the economy, based to a large extent on consciousness that even more rapid growth of productivity was being achieved in other developed countries; and various modifications of economic policy were proposed and experimented with, culminating in devaluation in November 1967.

The economics of wartime mobilization

There was very far from complete agreement about the economic management of the war. There were differences of opinion about the extent and urgency with which it was to be pursued: differences in some cases that were related to the need for labour and capital to accept what would be required of them by suspending their defence of their vested interests; and differences amongst politicians and administrators about how quickly it was feasible to press forward. But nobody believed what had been widely accepted in 1914, that the war could be fought on the basis of 'business as usual'.

The experience of the First World War had made it clear that sustained military effort required the backing of an economy well organized to achieve its objectives in the face of limited supplies of resources. This organization would require the supersession of the free enterprise economy, in which changes in the pattern of production were brought about by the effect of their experience of demand on the expectations of profit and loss of individual enterprises. For it could not be supposed that such an economy would respond quickly or strongly enough (even if the high levels of profit required had been politically acceptable).

The resources whose use would require central management were: manpower, where the direct needs of the armed forces had to be balanced by their indirect requirements for various types of skilled manpower embodied in munitions; particular materials, like special steels, the demand for which was likely to be disproportionately increased, or the supply of which, like rubber, might be interrupted. To some extent increased demand for materials, munitions, or machines could be met by imports, but the total supply of imports was limited by the country's ability to obtain overseas credit, and for most of the war was also limited by the carrying power of the merchant fleet in face of submarine attack.

This is not to say that there was complete agreement about the more specific details of these problems; or that the right answers were immediately, or in some cases ever, achieved. Sometimes sufficiently strong action had to await events that generated political resolution (and public acceptance). Events also required a reconsideration of strategies previously agreed. The fall of France in 1940 increased the length of supply routes and the rate of loss of ships. American provision of supplies without charge (Lend-Lease) removed the financial limitation on imports from the most important source of supply; and the entry of the United States into the war permitted a further specialization of functions with the United Kingdom concentrating more on repair work and the construction of an invasion base. And, of course, quite important shifts were required in response to military experience. Not all the changes were responses to such experience — some were themselves planned. Because the war had come earlier than expected (or the U.K.'s preparations for rearmament had begun late), the United Kingdom entered the war with inadequate productive capacity. There was therefore a phase in which machines and factories had to be constructed in order to increase the output of munitions in the future, and until the new factories were ready the full mobilization of manpower would have been impracticable.

It should be said that though the First World War had taught the lesson that a considerable degree of central control would be necessary, it did not present as administratively complex a problem as the Second World War. In the Second War the amount of equipment per head was larger, and typically it was more complex. The development of the war brought more changes in relative priorities, and weapons became obsolete more quickly.

The description given so far has presented the administration of the war economy solely in terms of 'the efficient allocation of resources' — a problem of correct economic calculation in a 'command economy'. But the problem of effective mobilization is more than that, for the effort of a man is not a physical constant that can be extracted in all circumstances. Service morale was thought to be sensitive to what was happening on the home front (with memories of what had happened in 1918 in Europe). Perhaps more important, home production, though it might be facilitated by the conscription of labour, needed to be supplemented by willing effort, that had to be sustained through what was expected to be a long war involving bombing. The contribution of poor industrial relations to the problems of production during the First World War was quite fresh in many memories.

In Parliamentary political terms this aspect of wartime administration is represented in the coalition government formed by Churchill in 1940; and, in particular, embodied in the inclusion of Ernest Bevin as Minister of Labour. But parliamentary near-unanimity was insufficient; there was also a careful tailoring of policies with civilian morale, particularly of manual workers, in mind. Bevin pursued (though he did not originate) the policy of 'voluntarism': labour was persuaded to abandon some restrictive practices and accept direction to particular employments. Conscription of labour for civilian purposes was extended only gradually, with each stage delayed until necessary, and the powers of direction used with moderation.

Other aspects of this strategy were the allocation of many consumables by rationing — and the maintenance of consumption at levels of nutrition sustainable for years. Indeed, while all civilians had to accept very many specific shortages, there was no attempt to call for the extreme abstention appropriate to a siege. Consumer expenditure in the middle of the war was still only 15 per cent below its pre-war level, and it seems likely that for many of the working class there was no fall at all. The sacrifice required from that class was of the additional spending power their increased potential bargaining power might otherwise have obtained for them. A closely related policy was the avoidance of inflation by price controls, subsidies on key essentials, as well as by financial policy for the avoidance of excess demand. Another related policy was the taxation of profits in excess of the 1939 level at 100 per cent; it was thought important to remove any fears of profiteering, despite the danger that this level of tax removed from managers any concern to minimize costs.

The populace was also promised a better future, with some actual legislation, notably the Education Act of 1944, being introduced, and other plans to improve social security and to maintain full employment being publicized. But it may be that as important as the explicit promises was the relationship between central government and people that was developed in wartime. Evacuation and other measures to deal with air raids required specific provision, while more generally the policies described and other aspects of the war effort required the efficient provision of information and its presentation to the population. Reinforced by the immediacy of the radio, the individual was made to feel that he was a part of a benevolent organization, and that his efforts and his sacrifices were being applied effectively to the war.

Wartime economic management

In some civil industries like textiles there were concentration schemes: the output of the industry was concentrated in particular mills working full-time, so that the reduced output could be produced with maximum efficiency, releasing labour and (in many cases) factory space for more important uses. On the railways, intervention involved the supersession of private companies by a unified government organization that administered the system, without regard for the interests of its parts, to accommodate the

new special demands, especially those related to military requirements. However, there was not time to reorganize all existing
services to achieve complete working integration. In some other
cases the functions of companies were suspended, and their assets
were requisitioned and administered as part of a single organization.

Expansion of war production was achieved in part by the
building of new government ordnance factories; but this method
was mainly confined to the producing of ammunition. Most of the
expansion was achieved by placing contracts with private companies which then received corresponding allocations of materials.
Sometimes, where new investment was required, the financial
resources would be supplied by the government, though the plant
would be built and managed by private companies. Usually there
was relatively little intervention in the actual management of
production. Sometimes the delegation of management to contractors involved their co-ordinating the production of components
with sub-contractors. Occasionally it extended to the development
of weapons: this might be the design of a weapon to meet a
requirement specified in general terms, of which a very successful
example was the Avro Lancaster; exceptionally, a company might
use its own resources to develop its own ideas about the feasibility
of which the government was sceptical — the de Haviland Mos-
quito.

The policy seemed to involve a lack of standardization and the
toleration of very different levels of efficiency in different firms. But
it would be wrong to interpret it either as doctrinaire subservience
to, or recognition of the superior merits of, private enterprise.
Primarily, it was a pragmatic policy taking account of the immediacy of need and realistically recognizing the time and uncertainty
involved in establishing new management organizations.

What, then, did constitute the 'control' of the economy? Basi-
cally it depended on the allocation of the various resources in short
supply, that is, materials and labour. This required the forecasting
of amounts that would be available, assessment of the amounts
required for various objectives, and allocation in accordance with
these objectives. In turn the outcome of an allocation required
checking so that waste did not result from imbalanced allocations

(for example, that there were enough propellers for aircraft) and that individual producers were not safeguarding their own efficiency by hoarding stocks.

To a very large extent the determination of civilian consumption by rationing, and of war and other categories of production by labour and material allocation, reduced the role of finance in economic management. The role of the Treasury in affecting expediture by the effect of its fiscal policies on disposable income, and by the effects of indirect taxes on the pattern of expenditure, was reduced. Similarly, the role of the banking system in influencing expenditure, particularly investment expenditure, was superseded by the direct control of investment; no investment for essential purposes was frustrated by lack of finance, because the government would always provide it, and virtually no investment was allowed for other purposes.

But, the question may be asked, 'Were not the incomes spent somewhere?' One answer is 'Not necessarily'. It is quite plausible to suppose that customers unable to get the goods they would have liked would decide to wait until after the war — provided they had confidence that money saved would not lose a substantial part of its value through inflation. People did in fact save a lot. The other answer was 'Yes, but the expenditure may make little demand on resources.' To take an extreme example: the fuller occupancy of cinemas simply created extra tax revenue, either in the form of extra entertainment duty or in the form of excess profits tax, whereas in peacetime the high profits would have attracted resources into the industry. In other cases, for example, tobacco and beer, the consumption of which increased significantly, there was some small demand on resources, but it was small because of the large element of indirect tax.

It was nevertheless of some importance that financial policy should reduce the amounts of money 'sloshing around', which might otherwise either have caused price inflation in non-controlled items (in turn creating a need for complex administration), or have tended to break down the discipline of rationing by creating black markets. It might even, to some extent, have diverted resources required for the war effort — though the former effects, and the need to avoid the disruption that would have been caused by accelerating inflation, were probably more important.

Two weapons existed for this purpose. The first was the encouragement of savings, to which extensive propaganda resources were applied; though it may be that 'War Weapons Weeks' were seen more as important for general morale than for their success in persuading individuals to exchange money for readily realizable securities. The second was increasing taxation. Rates of indirect and direct taxation were approximately doubled, and though there was caution in extending the incidence of direct taxation — tax rates on low incomes were very much less than they were to become twenty-five years later — a large number of wage-earners started to pay income tax for the first time. Initially, payment was secured by requiring employers to make weekly deductions that corresponded to tax liabilities on the previous year's income, but in 1943 this was modified so that employers made tax deductions related to the current level of income. This new system, P.A.Y.E. (Pay As You Earn), by reducing the pain of extraction of tax for wage-earners, significantly increased the taxable capacity of the country during the next thirty years.

At the end of the war it was widely accepted that it had been conducted efficiently, at least in its economic aspects, and that this had lessons for the management of the peacetime economy. In fact it is very difficult to find the criteria on which to base this sort of judgement. The rudimentary national accounts showed an increase in G.N.P. of twenty-five per cent by the middle of the war. But a period that involved such a drastic change in the pattern of output and where most of the increased output could only be valued by the payments made for it on a 'cost-plus' basis was not one that was really comparable with peacetime periods; at best the increase in G.N.P. is a measure of the increased *input* achieved by full employment, the conscription of women, and overtime. From 1941 onwards about fifty per cent of G.N.P. was devoted to the war effort — a level which matched that of Germany in 1941, and exceeded the forty per cent reached by the U.S.A. in 1944. Again, however, the measures are of input. We are measuring the very stiking political and administrative success of the government in mobilizing the efforts of the population for war purposes, and the sacrifices of the population; there is no measure of the efficiency with which the resources were used.

Although between 1939 and 1943 there were many examples of

large increases in war production, these were less spectacular than those achieved by the United States, or by Germany in the later stages of the war. The former comparison does not, however, allow for the cost of the continued changes in requirements on the U.K. economy, or for the fact that the U.K.–U.S. partnership involved, in the later stages of the war, a deliberate policy of concentrating production in the United States and switching some British manpower to maintain the strength of the Armed Forces.

It should be emphasized how rudimentary the 'planning' was in economic terms in comparison with what would be relevant to peacetime. Choices among the primary objectives, the relative numbers of tanks, ships, and aircraft to be produced, were made by the soldiers and politicians (although the newly developed discipline of Operations Research was providing some objective information on the relative effectiveness of weapons). The main job of the administrative machine was to avoid the confusion and waste that could have resulted from uncoordinated allocations, or the encouragement of activity in excess of supplies available. Avoidance of the waste of imperfect control rather than seeking low-cost recipes for meeting objectives was thus the important feature of economic planning. Although some thought had to be given to the next phase of the war, the time perspectives involved were very short indeed in comparison with those of peacetime.

This is not intended to imply that wartime planning was unnecessary, or that it was bad. Given the pressures of time available for its evolution it was bound to be imperfect. In war between States the infliction of chaos is as important as the infliction of wounds; and good staff-work that avoids chaos, particularly the chaos that is liable to accompany hasty mobilization and improvisation, could justifiably be regarded as a success.

The war then brought a shift in attitudes that was not quickly reversed. A great deal of 'informed opinion', particularly of civil servants and temporary civil servants, was no longer as sceptical of the efficiency of State management of the economy as it had been. At the basis of this view may have been a confusion between the effectiveness of the controls, that is, the fact that the decisions were carried out, and not disobeyed or evaded, and their efficiency — something much less perceptible. Among the population at large and the electorate, beliefs in the capacity of the State to manage the economy and find the 'right' answers, always widespread, had been powerfully reinforced by the State having for six years consciously cultivated the impression that indeed it had such benevolent omniscience.

The war had also enhanced the status of economists and economics. The success of economists in wartime administration was probably mainly due to a training that emphasizes that scarcities are relative to one another and to objectives, and that the principle of diminishing marginal utility is universal — providing a useful corrective to theories proposing recipes in more absolute terms. It may also have been due to their willingness to make the most of what fragmentary statistical information existed. But in what sense any economic theory (and in particular Keynesian theory) was proved by wartime experience is much less clear.

Control and planning in the post-war world

There were several sources of high potential demand for the output of the post-war economy in addition to a need for higher exports. The government, although intending considerable demobilization, did not intend an immediate reversion to the unarmed state of the early 1930s. Retaining ambitions to be a power that counted, it was committed not only to sizeable forces but also to continue to supply those forces with newly-developed weapons, the most spectacular example being the development of an independent atomic bomb. In addition, the Labour Government entered office committed to a wide range of objectives. Some of these, like nationalization or the Health Service, probably involved no immediate demand on resources that would not have occurred even if the ownership of the industries had not changed. But others, particularly housing and school-building, were given a high priority. Industry, despite its expansion of capacity, had accumulated worn and obsolescent plant and large reserves intended to finance replacement. The consumer not only had the spending power implicit in his current earnings, but also, in many cases, had accumulated from the war savings that were not intended to be kept as savings permanently.

Logically the main method of control should have been by the allocation of the resource in short supply, that is, labour. But such controls involved undesirable reductions in personal freedom that would not be accepted for long. After the War there was no compulsory transfer of labour into occupations where it was scarce (with the exception of the mines as an alternative to military service) though until March 1950 the Control of Engagements Order was used to prevent movement away from what were considered important industries.

The need to keep imports below a level which would have permitted the unrestricted use of materials, together with shortages of home-produced materials like steel, also left in government hands a means of exercising control over the pattern of output. But such controls could last only as long as the materials were in short supply. To maintain them artificially in short supply indefinitely would have been undesirable and impractical. It was undesirable because it led to a waste of resources by firms attempting to economize on the use of the material at the expense of other materials or labour. And impracticable because the effective operation of controls depended to a great extent on the willingness of industrialists to accept them and not try to evade or discredit them; and also because in many cases the controls were in fact administered by men seconded from business. The longer such physical controls had been maintained, the more likely it would be that either they would have had virtually no real effect, or, possibly, that they might have been transferred, in effect, into a mechanism for enforcing restrictive arrangements to maintain the market shares of the larger members of the industries affected.

Direct controls could be used to contribute towards the accomplishment of broad objectives where there was sufficient agreement on objectives. Thus preferences in the allocation of materials to firms engaged in exports helped the export drive in a period when the strategy was to shift resources into exports. But the control could not be used more finely. In wartime, the government as customer made the judgement which weapons it was most important to produce; it did not possess comparable detailed knowledge that could be used to maximize export earnings from given resources. As it was, it was indeed an important question whether, in a situation where exporters exported out of obligation and in an atmosphere where there was disapproval of profits, a great deal of foreign currency revenue may not have been lost because they felt no pressure to obtain the best possible prices for their products. Even where the government could discern priorities in more detail, for example, the need to export to the dollar area, it was difficult to enforce such priorities without risking damage to the objective of increasing exports generally. Such enforcement would have required exact detailed knowledge of the opportunities available in the dollar area and of the feasibility of particular producers adjusting themselves to supply them.

Consumption could be restrained by rationing on the principle of the simple fairness of equal shares — so long as severe restraint was visibly necessary. But as the particular causes of shortages were removed, how was it to be determined which commodities should be rationed tightly and which loosely? In other cases efficient control was endangered by the unwillingness of ministers to recognize the limits to the resource available. Thus, for example, the efficiency of building operations was reduced and the output of the industry was actually less than it might have been because of the issuing of an excessive number of licences for house-building, etc. by Bevan in 1947.

During the early part of the post-war period there was a great deal of talk about 'planning' — but successive Economic Surveys made increasingly cautious and tentative references to the process, and it must be doubted whether there was any successful development of the techniques of co-ordinating detailed forecasts and determining detailed requirements in peacetime conditions (as distinct from the macro-economic forecasting discussed later). Even if there had been sufficient accurate detailed information available about the current state of the economy, there would not have been available techniques that could have made elaborate projections based upon them. The precipitation of the economy into a 'fuel crisis' in 1947 and the failure to realize the extent to which the rearmament programme of 1950 would draw resources from exports and investment, because of the demand for metals and engineering products, were errors that suggest a government machine that, either through administrative incompetence or political wilfulness, was incapable of relatively simple calculations.

Many detailed controls were already being abolished by the Labour Government (Harold Wilson's 'bonfire of controls' was in

1948) and it is difficult to say how much the change in government in 1951 increased the pace of the process that would have accelerated once the acute pressures brought by the Korean War had passed. With the apparatus of control dismantled, no element of 'planning' remained. This was not because the Conservative Government discontinued it, but simply because nothing of significance corresponding to that label had existed.

The ascendancy of Keynesianism

The main conclusion that Keynes and Keynesians drew from his *General Theory of Employment* (1936) was that unemployment of labour could be due to a persistent general deficiency of demand. In such circumstances the policy advocated by some of cutting wages would be irrelevant, if not positively harmful, because to cut wages would still further reduce demand. The implied policy counterpart of this explanation of unemployment was that the level of employment could be increased by official financial policy: to some, but not necessarily a sufficient, extent, by monetary policy, that is, low interest rates and easy credit; more certainly, either by increasing government expenditure relative to revenue or alternatively by the reduction of taxation. The diagnosis of demand deficiency was not inconsistent with the simultaneous existence of structural unemployment, that is, unemployment concentrated among labour in specific trades from which it had difficulty in moving. But it might well be that with a higher level of demand structural unemployment would be reduced, because the barriers to the transfer of labour from the declining industries would prove less substantial than they had done when there was a general surplus of labour.

Keynes' *General Theory* was primarily a piece of economic logic, and its central contribution was negative; that is, it rebutted arguments that had seemed to establish that there were strong natural forces that could normally be relied upon to maintain full employment in an economy. It did show that, in principle, government budgetary policy could be effective in increasing employment. But the practicability of such policies could not be demonstrated merely by argument; and the *General Theory* itself stopped a long way short even of providing a blueprint for action (and was indeed curiously distant from the particular problems of the U.K. in the 1930s).

During the War, Keynesian views acquired increasing acceptance. Though nothing in that period could directly demonstrate the success of Keynesian policies in dealing with unemployment, Keynes himself in *How to Pay for the War* (1940) adapted his method of thinking to the problems of excess demand. As we have argued, it is difficult to assess quite how important the resulting financial policy was to the primary objectives of the War, but nothing happened to cast doubt on the possibility of using financial policy to manage the level of demand. Official national income accounting was pioneered, and seemed to provide an important administrative tool for the Keynesian management of demand. And both Keynesian theory and national income accounting provided impressive intellectual stiffening for the unofficial 'Beveridge Report' on full employment (1944). 'Full employment', obviously an attractive policy, became for many administrators and politicians an objective that would be feasible in the post-war world.

The acceptance of Keynesian policies stemmed from a victory in intellectual debate, but was not entirely a triumph of reason. The qualifications inherent in its logical foundations were either not perceived or thought undeserving of emphasis by its apostles; while for many it was acceptable simply because it seemed to endorse the propriety of a high level of spending and to overthrow the uncomfortable 'balanced budget' doctrines of the previous financial orthodoxy.

Keynesian policies also brought changes in the content of economics as taught and studied, producing in turn amongst the new generation of the rapidly growing profession a different way of looking at the world. Up to a point this was desirable. Keynesian macro-economics dealt directly with the behaviour of economic aggregates, like national income, consumption, or investment; and it involved relationships between these aggregates that were not readily perceptible from consideration of the behaviour of individual firms and industries — an approach that had perhaps been overemphasized in British economics since 1870. But the shift could be taken too far. There was a danger that heeding the advice of economists would be rather like handing over the conduct of battle to students of military history who think of armies as really being composed of the precisely delimited, uniformly motivated, units fully portrayed by the conventional symbols used to represent them on maps. In fact the management of economic policy was never handed over to economists; and one of their most important roles was to react critically to the spontaneous, naïve, and often inconsistent theorizing of politicians and civil servants. And, moreover, experience of economic management generally inoculated economists against over-enthusiasm for the abstract intricacies of academic economics as it was to develop after Keynes. Nevertheless, the fundamental simplifications of economics, often unspelt, reinforced the natural inclinations of administrators in creating a presumption of the ultimate manageability of the economy, for which, in fact, there was no substantial basis in experience.

Thus Keynesian policy, or at least the policies of the government that were called 'Keynesian' (for with Keynes's premature death in 1946 it is a matter of speculation what policies he would have approved of), though never unanimously accepted, dominated official and academic thought in the U.K. for about two decades. Subsequently, from the later sixties thoroughgoing opposition grew; while more generally other qualifications and limitations of the simple post-war Keynesiansim were accepted.

When we say that 'Keynesian' policies were pursued, we refer to two related but not identical things. Firstly, we refer to a willingness to use government expenditure and, more especially, government taxation to affect the aggregate level of effective demand — fiscal policy. Put over-simply this meant having a budget surplus if it was desired to reduce the demand of the private sector ('over-simply' because it was never assumed either that every type of taxation was equivalent in its effect on demand per pound of revenue or that a pound of revenue simply cancelled a pound of expenditure). Secondly, we refer to reliance on the importance of the Keynesian relationship between income and expediture when making predictions of the way the economic situation would change, especially as a consequence of budgetary changes. This led to an almost exclusive concern with the entities that were included in the National Income accounts — and further, to a concern with them in 'real' terms.

This willingness to use fiscal policy was generally associated with an unwillingness to rely on, or even to use, 'monetary' instruments, that is, control of the monetary supply through Central Bank action — particularly where this involved increasing the rate of interest. There were several reasons for this unwillingness. Keynes himself had come to believe that 'monetary' weapons were inadequate to deal with slumps; but many Keynesians went further, and denied that they would be effective in restraining demand — being very much influenced by what businessmen said about the effect of the rate of interest. Keynes also believed that it took a long time to reduce the long-term rate of interest. If, as many Keynesians, influenced by the gloomier passages of the *General Theory*, believed, a recurrence of the inter-war depression was likely in the middling future, it was desirable to keep the rate of interest low. Whether or not such gloomy expectations were general, it is fair to claim that nobody anticipated the very high level of investment demand that would be sustained for the next twenty years. Nor was it anticipated that low interest rates would be effectively lowered further by inflation. Other Keynesians thought it desirable to keep interest rates low in order to prevent the distribution of income moving in favour of rentiers. Alternatively they wished to keep down the interest burden of the National Debt.

To some extent the denial of a use for a monetary policy was a matter of the use of words. The ascendant Keynesians determined the vocabulary, and for them 'fiscal policy' was defined to include the running of a government surplus or deficit. The fact that such a deficit or surplus had implications for the financial markets was not adequately considered.

In the immediate post-war period reliance was placed exclusively on fiscal policy; although government expenditure fell sharply with demobilization, there was little reduction of taxation rates and government revenue was the same proportion of G.N.P. in 1948 as it was in 1945 (33·8 per cent). The result was that the wartime government deficit was converted into a significant surplus. Monetary controls (that is, the Capital Issues Committee and the restriction of bank advances) were retained, but until 1951 monetary policy was not used in a restrictive way. Indeed, under Dalton's chancellorship (1945–7) there was an attempt to force long-term rates of interest below the very low levels that had been achieved during the War. Holders of long-term securities were not convinced that the attempt would be successful and took the opportunity to move into shorter-term securities or cash. Whether or not this had much immediate effect on demand is doubtful, but it did aggravate the problems of monetary control subsequently.

Conservative chancellors proved more willing to use monetary policy for restrictive purposes, the first occasion being in October 1951 when bank rate was raised to 2½ per cent and 'made effective' at that level, and some of the debt was funded — the primary intention of which was to dissuade the commercial banks and other financial institutions from extending credit to the private sector. Conservative policy in the 1950s may have used a wider range of weapons, but it would be difficult to claim that it was more effective in macro-economic control. The mixture of monetary and fiscal policies seems to have been not so much a skilful blending as a haphazard alternation between two sources of advice: the Keynesian advice of the Treasury and that of bankers. The limit of absurdity was reached in 1955 when it seems to have been supposed that it was appropriate to tighten 'monetary' policy to permit fiscal slackening by the reduction of taxes. Most of the protagonists of monetary policy in the 1950s, while implicitly emphasizing the importance of money, were mainly concerned to advocate a role for the Central Bank in intelligently using its various financial weapons to assist with managing the economy. Few were monetarists in the sense of the later 1960s: they did not believe that the Central Bank's role could be reduced to setting a target for the money supply on the basis of an automatic rule.

The report of the Radcliffe Committee on the Monetary System (1959) provided an authoritative updated description of the institutions of the financial system and of the role of the National Debt. Unfortunately the experience of the previous fifteen years, when the company sector had been abnormally flush with cash and liquid balances, and in many cases had few worries about profitability, provided inadequate evidence of the potential effectiveness of monetary weapons. The Committee may, too, have been over-academic in reporting an inconclusive debate about whether it was money in some narrow sense or liquidity in some broader sense that the government should seek to control. In the medium run, its stimulus led to a great improvement in statistics on monetary and financial matters, which was itself a factor leading to the eventual recognition that monetary policy had an important role to play; but, in the short run, its inconclusiveness was taken as a licence for believing that money was of no importance.

Whether or not the main reliance should have been placed on fiscal or monetary policy is a quite different matter from the neglect of 'monetary variables' in the observation of the economy. The *General Theory* made a contribution by stressing the likely causal importance of variables like income and investment and consumption — a contribution enhanced by the creators of the National Income Accounts. But it was never shown that, in the actual management of the economy, observation of what was happening could be confined to these variables. It seems likely that the neglect of information about money reflected a dogmatic view that 'money is not important', though it may also be the case that there was no very easy way of incorporating it in the system of forecasting that was evolving. There was also a neglect, in the forecasting apparatus, of the effects of companies' financial position on their investment.

The 'External Constraint'

In the management of the U.K. economy from the end of the War until 1977, the balance-of-payments seemed continually to constrain the freedom of action of governments and, with few exceptions, provided a crisis every other year which required emergency action.

One type of problem an economy may face because of its involvement in international trade is a lack of demand for its exports — products for which capital equipment has been constructed and for which labour has acquired special skills. These resources become unemployed, and their reduced incomes may produce further loss of employment elsewhere in the economy. Such unemployment had been the principal cause on the cycles experienced by the U.K. for almost a century before 1939 and was a major cause of the longer inter-war depression. Its recurrence after the War was feared, but it was never a significant problem, partly because of the steady growth of the external world and partly because many fewer parts of the U.K. industry were so exclusively dependent on exports.

The second type of problem occurs when an economy has its own currency and the flows of demand to exchange it into foreign currencies to make external payments do not match the flows which supply foreign currency: the balance-of-payments problem. The solution of this requires *either* an alteration of exchange rates *or* some measures to reduce the demand for foreign currency, measures which may include contraction of internal demand. Such balance-of-payments crises had happened before the War (notably 1931) but never as often as they happened after the War (1947, 49, 51, 55, 57, 61, 64–7, 68, 73–6).

With some less developed countries, the balance-of-payments is a continuous problem; the supply of foreign currency is always less than the demand for it. The U.K.'s problem took a different form because sterling was a currency which overseas nationals and institutions were often willing to use for trading or holding as reserves. Crises took the form of waves of lack of confidence which caused these foreign users hurriedly to reduce their holdings of Sterling (a 'run on the bank') because they feared that the value of Sterling in terms of other foreign currencies would have to be reduced. In 1949 such speculation was successful in forcing a devaluation of the pound from the parity of $4·03 adopted at the beginning of the War to $2·80 — the level at which it was maintained until 1967.

In the first ten or fifteen years after the War, the liability of the U.K. to speculative pressure could be partially ascribed to the War itself, when she had financed purchases of materials and the expenditure of her armies overseas by payments of sterling which had vastly augmented the balances held in pre-war London by the Sterling Area countries. Subsequently, with the growth in volume of trade and inflation and a certain amount of repayment, the size of these balances became less important, but the pound continued to be vulnerable to the opinions of short-run creditors because, from the later fifties, British financial institutions attracted loans repayable on demand or short notice with relatively high interest rates. To some extent Britain was borrowing short to lend long as she had been doing in the 1920s.

In contemporary demonology this exposed the U.K. to the whims of short-term creditors. The economy moved forward jerkily (by 'stop–go' motion) because governments had abruptly, and consequently wastefully, to 'put on the brakes' by imposing deflationary policies, simply because the 'Gnomes of Zurich' decided not to continue holding pounds. In borrowing short, the country was certainly being exposed to this sort of risk. But to suppose that the apparent wastes of 'stop–go' were *caused* by the exposed international financial position, is to suppose that the trends of the British economy that were perceived by the external creditors did not exist; or that governments could have continued on the same course for other reasons. Only the crisis of 1957 had no foundation in the internal state of the economy.

At first sight the small sizes of the balance-of-payments deficits (and indeed the frequent surpluses) belie the existence of a balance-of-payments problem before the 1960s. But two points must be made. First, the statistics themselves apply to whole years, and therefore usually include the effects of corrective action in response to the balance-of-payments crises as well as the crisis itself. Projection of the rate of deficit emerging just before the crises might give a different impression. Second, the position was not as favourable as the statistics suggest. Many of the U.K.'s exports in the 1950s were paid for with the accumulated sterling debts from the War, and also many exports were made on credit. In neither case was foreign currency being currently received. Moreover, a good deal of the 'earnings' of U.K. overseas investments could not be remitted to the U.K. without damaging the future of the business, or in some cases because of overseas exchange control (and, indeed, by the normal conventions of national income accounting, these overseas earnings were exaggerated because insufficient allowance was made for capital consumption and stock appreciation).

In the period from the end of the War to 1951 it was not surprising that there was a balance-of-payments problem. In 1938 there had been a deficit that was too large to be maintained indefinitely. Since then there had been a loss of earnings because of the enforced sale of foreign investments to pay for imports before Lend-Lease was introduced in 1941, and because a great deal of the merchant fleet had been sunk. And the terms of trade (ratio of export to import prices) had moved sharply against the U.K. The net result was that by 1950 balance on current account, with imports severely controlled to 70 per cent of their 1938 volume, required 175 per cent of the 1938 volume of exports. Though pent-up world demand and the absence of German and Japanese competition made this feasible as a selling problem, there was required for its achievement a large shift of resources into producing exports.

As Figure 1.2 shows, subsequently to 1951 the terms of trade swung back, at first rapidly, then more slowly in the later sixties, finally to turn very abruptly against the U.K. after 1973 (primarily but not solely because of the increased price of oil). The effect in the 1950s was profound: even when import controls were relaxed, and finally removed, the proportion of the G.D.P. spent on imports was lower than it had been in the early fifties. Given that the balance-of-payments was benefiting from the improvement of the terms of trade to the extent of £100 million a year between 1951 and 1961, it is not surprising that the crises became deeper in the middle 1960s when the terms of trade failed to continue improving so rapidly. The fact that balance-of-payments crises continued in the 1950s is especially notable, and must be primarily attributed to a slackening of the 'export drive' of 1945–50.

There was a distinct slackening in the growth of exports after 1950. While for the rest of the world exports grew more rapidly than industrial production, for the United Kingdom from 1950 to 1967 they grew more slowly. Initially, in the short run, substantial blame can be put on the Korean War which diverted to domestic rearmament substantial resources in the metal and engineering industries. Subsequently the end of raw material control removed a pressure on manufacturers to export in preference to supplying the home market. But many would see the persistence of the trend for fifteen years simply as evidence of loss of competitiveness, witnessed by a rapid decline in the U.K.'s share of the world manufacturing market, and caused primarily by a failure of manufacturing productivity to rise sufficiently rapidly relative to increasing wages, to match changes in wage costs elsewhere.

It should, however, be noted that the slackened rate of growth of exports was not, in the medium run, accompanied by any significant growth of general unemployment and excess capacity in the economy (apart from sectors like Lancashire cotton where there were special reasons for long-term decline). Other claims on resources, particularly consumers expenditure but increasingly also domestic investment and government expenditure, had been allowed to take the place of exports. Indeed there may be an even more direct connection. It was generally accepted that, as domestic demand increased, there would naturally be an increased demand for materials and components to be embodied in the final output; this would imply a roughly proportionate increase in the demand for imports. What was not so expected was that, as the level of home demand increased, a more than proportionate increase in demand for imports would occur as users found home produced goods in short supply and, similarly, that exports would be delivered less quickly if their makers were having to cope with an increased volume of domestic orders. Indeed, although these effects are perfectly compatible with a Keynesian view, some Keynesian forecasters were very sceptical of their existence because they did not fit the actual 'models' used — though these models seem to have led to consistently over-optimistic expectations about the balance of trade. Such effects, moreover, would not necessarily be reversed as soon as domestic demand was curbed; once imports had been attracted in, market contacts between customer and supplier were established which both might well be reluctant to abandon; while delivery delays in exports, once experienced, would diminish the attractiveness of U.K. goods. To what extent the long-term trading decline is attributable to these causes has not been established.

In the immediate post-war period the 'export drive' was supplemented by a continuation of controls introduced in wartime; the general controls on the use of foreign currency by U.K. citizens together with controls on the use of some of the sterling balances; and controls on imports. Possibly because of a desire to maintain the goodwill of the other sterling area countries, and because, ostensibly, purchases from or loans to them involved no direct depletion of the currency resources, imports from sterling area countries were subject to few restrictions, and while there was control on the making of new issues in the London capital market there was a fairly large flow of funds to the Commonwealth. Import controls were tightened in 1951 because of the Korean War, but subsequently they were relaxed by stages until by 1960 virtually no controls remained on the import of goods (although a limit remained on the amount that could be spent by U.K. tourists overseas). Controls did remain on the 'export of capital' and these, in fact, were tightened by the extension of the restriction of port-folio investment to all parts of the sterling area, first in 1968 by informal pressure on financial institutions, and subsequently in 1971, by simple prohibition of net additions to portfolios. The 1960s did see, in the import surcharge of 1964 and the import deposit scheme of 1968, measures to impede imports that might be described as controls. Neither, however, involved direct restric-tion, and both essentially worked by increasing the cost of imports.

With the removal of direct controls on trade, British industry still retained in the U.K. market the very substantial levels of protection that had been introduced between 1914 and 1939 and the effect of this in permitting much higher levels of profit in the home market than were obtainable overseas may have reinforced the caution of British businesses in expanding their businesses in the later 1950s and early 1960s.

However, the phase of very high protection was temporary. Successive negotiations reduced many of the tariffs operating be-tween developed countries to quite low levels — though this left other impediments (conformity of imports to certain standards, for the sake of health, safety, standardization, and simply bureauc-racy) to the flow of goods. In addition Britain, having failed to join the European Economic Community (then The Six), became a founder member of the European Free Trade Area in 1959.

It may seem paradoxical that the U.K. should have played a leading role in international agreements, and generally adhered to them in spirit as well as letter, despite frequent balance-of-payments crises. Political factors, particularly her commitments to the United States embodied in the I.M.F. and GATT agreements, may have been important in this. There may also have been a realization that although, by comparison with the United States, Britain had achieved relative prosperity in the 1930s, and that, in part, this had been due to a willingness to use both tariffs and competitive currency depreciation, there had been an incipient balance-of-payments crisis in the late 1930s despite very favoura-ble terms of trade. In the post-war world neither the favourable terms of trade nor the special role of the U.K. as industrial supplier to the Sterling Area could be expected to be repeated. In the last resort, the United Kingdom needed to make substantial imports, and she stood more chance of paying for these in a world in which the general volume of trade was growing most rapidly on a non-discriminating basis than if countries resorted to protection and bilateral agreements.

It is significant that the long-term liberalization met with relatively little opposition from vested interests. This confirms the impression of a fully-employed economy with business on the whole content with the demand and profits it encountered. It is also difficult for manufacturers to complain about absence of protection if they are losing market shares through failure to match delivery, or, in some cases, because of failure to design products best suited to customers' needs. The most significant exception was the Lancashire cotton industry, which faced competition based on the cheap prices at which developing countries like Hong Kong were willing to supply. Here quota restrictions (subsequently tariff and quota) were imposed on grounds of disruption, that is, the rate of growth of imports was causing an unacceptably rapid rate of decline of the domestic industry.

'Liberalization' was accompanied by an acceptance of the implications of the rise of multi-national business. Though the process was supervised, no restrictive control was exercised on the immigration of overseas enterprise and it was accepted that such businesses would have considerable freedom both in remitting profits to their parents, and in switching their resources from one company to another. Development overseas by British companies was subjected to much more restriction when it involved an actual 'export of capital'; companies being encouraged to finance new overseas operations by borrowing overseas. Investment by the retention of earnings overseas was subject to less restraint; and would, in any case, have been virtually impossible to control.

The management of the economy

Apart from three months when the hard winter of 1963 caused physical disruption, there was only one month between 1948 and 1968 when the rate of unemployment reached three per cent — a level which Keynes and wartime planners would have regarded as full employment; most of the time unemployment was very much less.

Figure 8.1 Fluctuations in unemployment and real output 1938–75

Note: Deviation of G.D.P. from trend is the percentage by which actual G.D.P. varied from what it would have been if it had grown constantly (at the average rate of growth between 1948 and 1971). Unemployment is plotted inversely to facilitate direct comparison with the deviation of G.D.P. We would expect low rates of unemployment to be associated with positive deviations of G.D.P.

Such a long sustained level of full employment was unprecedented, and it tended to be taken for granted that it was the consequence of the pursuit of Keynesian policies. But it is very difficult to maintain that the expectations of wartime about the need for deficit finance in the post-war period were fulfilled. There had been no appreciation at all of the scale of opportunities for private investment in fixed capital that would be associated with post-war industrial growth; and there may well have been an under-estimation of the personal sector's capacity to spend its own savings on house construction. On the other hand, the high level of government expenditure (even when not financed by borrowing) augmented demand in so far as it caused private saving, by high taxation, to be less than it would otherwise have been. And though, as public utilities, the nationalized industries could have been large borrowers and investors, it is unlikely that they would have been as large borrowers and spenders as they were if they had not been in government ownership. In so far as the high level of employment was related to the high level of government expenditure, rather than to the size of the deficit, it becomes less easy to say how far the high level of employment was due to *policies* to maintain it as such and how far a by-product of other policies.

It might also be argued that private investment would not have been undertaken to the extent that it was without the confident expectation that governments would intervene successfully to prevent cumulative depressions from emerging. There is no doubt, too, that if we consider particular years of recovery, substantial expansions in demand were produced by government policies on the basis of Keynesian calculations. However, this is to look at the matter too selectively; for the recoveries so promoted were not recoveries from natural depressions but from recessions induced by government management.

At most it can be argued that demand may have been rather higher than it would have been if the government had pursued pre-Keynesian principles. The problems of economic management were, then, those of a naturally fairly fully-employed economy: to exercise some influence on the allocation of output between investment, government, personal consumption, and exports, and to steer a course that avoided fluctuations.

Between 1946 and 1951 real consumption expenditure grew by less than 1.2 per cent per annum, whilst from 1951 to 1964 it grew by 2·9 per cent. A parallel calculation shows that whereas the growth in exports from 1946 to 1951, both to offset the losses of the War and the adverse movement of the terms of trade that continued in the post-war period, required a diversion *into* exports of resources that would have permitted a doubling of the growth of consumer expenditure, in the period 1951 to 1964 the favourable movement of the terms of trade made available sufficient resources to account for more than a quarter of the observed growth. These calculations do not tell the whole story: not all the resources were derived from or allocated to consumption; and the statistics do not measure the many advantages consumers found in moving from rationing, austerity, and the tyranny of a sellers market. Nevertheless the calculations do constitute a strong prima facie case that most of the most obvious contrast between the two periods can be attributed to an exogeneous factor, the terms of trade, the change in direction of which coincided with the change from Labour to Conservative government.

This is not to imply that the switch in resources that occurred was brought about by positive government policy. Although there was some reduction in rates of taxation, and there was a switch from a surplus to a deficit in the overall position of the public sector, the share of consumption in G.D.P. declined fairly steadily through the whole period of Conservative government. What did happen in the 1950s was that because of the favourable change in the terms of trade (and because of the fall in the relative price of manufactured consumption goods) the *real* value of consumption changed more favourably than its money value would indicate. Government action was essentially negative — it did not attempt the politically difficult task of raising taxes to remove part of this gain from consumers as it would have needed to do if either the rate of growth of exports or investment had been higher.

The government did not seem very capable of avoiding quite sharp fluctuations in economic activity. Althoug the variations in unemployment were not very large, variations in the rate of growth of G.D.P. were much larger, from 0 per cent in a recession to 5 per cent in a boom. At the time there was a great deal of concern about the wastes caused by 'stop–go'. Such complaints were in part a product of political competition — perfectionist criticisms by an opposition in a democracy where it had been widely accepted that a government could control the economy. They were also a natural product of a country with subsidiary bureaucracies (of firms as well as public bodies) that complained if they felt it would be advantageous — in perfectly good faith because they knew that they could be more efficient if allowed to have a smoothly evolving situation, and would invest more if they experienced no nasty shocks to their expectations. It was suggested that desire to give tax concessions and increase incomes at times when general elections were pending, concessions that had subsequently to be reversed, contributed to the instability; but the cycles could also be explained by inadequacies in the apparatus for economic forecasting. However, from a more distant perspective, it is difficult to attach very great importance to the matter, except for the evidence it provides of the practical limits of government competence. Some of the U.K.'s faster growing rivals experienced cycles that were quite as severe as those of the U.K.

Seen in retrospect, the most serious deficiency of the period was the failure of British industrial growth to match the performance of trading rivals. For some years after the War no special priority was given to industrial investment which, allowing for the exceptional rise in price of capital goods during the War, was no higher than it had been in 1938. A lot of industrial capacity had been created during the War; and the production of capital goods competed either with exports, in the case of engineering, or housing, in the case of building. There was perhaps no realization of the rate of growth of output that would become possible in the post-war period and consequently of the proportion of G.D.P. that ought to be invested. Possibly there was also a belief that, when, as was expected, a slump arrived, investment could be encouraged as a means of taking up the slack. (It certainly seems that some types of public investment were postponed for this reason.)

By the mid-fifties the greater rates of progress of other countries were becoming apparent. Initially this could reasonably be ascribed to a 'catching-up' from very low levels, but as the growth was sustained this explanation became increasingly less convincing. By the later fifties there was fairly wide agreement that the poorer performance of the U.K. was attributable to its lower rate of investment. There was also increasing consciousness that other countries' export prices were rising more slowly than those of the U.K. In the other countries export prices were rising more slowly than domestic prices — suggesting that in part the effect was the consequence of the reaping of economies of scale in the export industries. This was noticed by some observers who emphasized the possibility of breaking into a 'virtuous circle' of increasing exports and increasing economies of scale in manufacturing, thus sustaining growth. However, the initiation of such a process required a halting of the process whereby wage demands dragged wage costs upwards.

One result of unease with the country's performance was a revival of interest in economic planning — stimulated in part by the apparent success of the French in devising a role for planning in an economy that continued to be dominated by private enterprise. The revival of planning, embodied in 1962 in the creation of the National Economic Development Council (N.E.D.C.) supported by the National Economic Development Office (N.E.D.O.), sought to raise the growth of the economy by discussion: of the obstacles to growth that were perceived by individual industries; and of the implications for the demand of different industries of achieving higher rates of growth in the hope that the vision of opportunities so created would itself increase the willingness to invest. The Labour Government of 1964 gave the process greater urgency by incorporating the planning team in the new Department of Economic Affairs; the N.E.D.C. and N.E.D.O. surviving as a general forum for discussion, with the 'little Neddies' for each industry playing the same role.

Some would see the Plan which was produced in 1965 as having been smothered by Civil Service apathy and finally extinguished by an assertion of older Treasury policies in the deflation of 1966. Others would see it as having destroyed itself. It's fundamental weakness was the political role it had acquired. Trades unions were represented on the N.E.D.C., because plans for investment and increasing productivity seemed likely to require their co-operation. But, with the failure of the Conservative Government to achieve acceptance by the unions of a separate National Incomes Commission, the N.E.D.C. and its Plan became involved in the attempt to solve the problem of wage inflation. The T.U.C. started with a presumption that planning could bring large gains, and was also interested in establishing a high target which could be used as a norm for the wage increases that could be given. The growth rate that emerged could be seen to be a target imposed by what seemed like union-government negotiations, not as based on a dispassionate and realistic survey of possibilities — and was consequently less credible for its original purpose.

It must also be doubted whether, in any case, much could have emerged from the Plan. In the balance-of-payments crises of the 1950s, certain identifiable physical factors, for example, a shortage of steel, seemed of crucial importance; but it is not clear that all the problems of growth could be seen in such physical terms. Although, with the aid of the power of modern computers, it had become feasible to make much more detailed input-output calculations, it was unclear how much confidence could be attached to them. More fundamentally, in an economy that had to be flexible in face of changing world conditions and changing technology, it is doubtful how far it was desirable to seem to give the management of companies a promise of smooth conditions. Planning that did not include a realistic indication of the contingencies that might arise, and of the consequent adaptation required of its participants, could do more harm than good. There was indeed a significant danger that planning might simply provide a forum in which powerful interests pursued their search for security, obtaining promises either at the expense of pushing all burdens of adjustment onto others or at the risk of subsequent disillusion when the undertakings were repudiated.

The dominant assumption at the time continued to be that investment leading to growth of productivity would best be stimulated by demand, and this led to the Maudling boom of 1964–66 (though continued expansion had to be curbed because of a balance-of-payments crisis in 1964, unemployment remained very low and the pressure on resources high, until positively deflationary action was taken in 1966). A large part of the reflation was based on new programmes of public expenditure — a response to the view that in the economic growth of the 1950s expenditure on hospitals, higher education, and roads had failed to keep in step with private consumption (Galbraith's 'private affluence and public squalor') and the direct employment given by this left little room for further expansion. These characteristics of the 1964 boom cannot be blamed specifically on the Chancellor, Maudling. He was nevertheless responsible for the strategy of 'going for growth' — the belief that reflation, though it initially might bring a balance-of-payments deficit, would ultimately induce enough investment and that this in turn would enable the balance-of-payments to be restored. This was based on a generalization of a widespread opinion by businessmen that 'export growth' could only be based on a 'healthy home market'. What was never explained was how, in the medium future, when the investment induced by the boom became productive, it would result in a restoration of the balance-of-payments sufficient to allow for a continuation of growth, if the spare capacity that was available in 1962 (which was itself the product of the preceding boom) had not been so used. The Maudling boom seems in retrospect rather like a First World War plan for an attack — an assumption that willingness to incur heavy losses was sufficient to ensure success.

It could be argued that the Maudling attack failed because it was insufficiently single-minded; and that much of the increase in demand came from an increase in public expenditure, which although desirable in itself in the long run, limited the scope for an

expansion of manufacturing and exports that would have constituted a basis for a self-sustaining acceleration of growth, because of
the economies of scale and growth obtainable in manufacturing. A
way to break into this 'virtuous circle' of self-sustaining growth
would have been to obtain the stimulating increase in demand
from exports by devaluation.

Such a strategy depended on the existence of some unemployed
resources capable of supplying the extra demand and accepted the
common assumption that there was significant underemployment
in the economy. It is true that, as measured by unemployment,
there was in the recessions of the late fifties and early sixties more
spare capacity than there had been. But much of this was
associated with structural change, the decline of coal production,
the end of the long boom in shipbuilding, and the decline of
textiles, and it was questionable how far this would have been
readily available to meet the extra demand that an export-led
boom would have created.

What this proposed stategy ignored was that during the 1950s
many of the sectors producing capital goods had remained fully
employed and that increasing demand would once again make
acute the shortages of crucial materials and components which
frustrated efficient production in other firms — the 'bottlenecks'
that had plagued the economy in the immediate post-war period.
Because of the availability of imported supplies, the bottlenecks
would not be as acute as they had been (this itself was liable to
create a balance-of-payments problem), but there would remain
many areas in the construction industries where imports could not
do much to relieve them. The behaviour of firms faced with such
difficulties is not uniform. For some, encountering shortages may
be a challenge evoking determined and ingenious adaptation;
perhaps this was the German case with appetites of managements
for growth fed by several years of vigorous expansion previously
unconstrained by acute labour shortage. But there were few
grounds for such an optimistic presumption about the British
economy, whose managers had been worn down by twenty years of
coping with the problems of excess demand.

There was, too, in this strategy an unquestioning acceptance of
the assumption that had accompanied the Keynesian revolution
— of the almost exclusive importance of fiscal policies that oper-

ated on broad aggregates like consumption or investment: or, perhaps operated indirectly on investment via control of the over-all level of demand. It was assumed that the process of growth, which after all appears to involve enterprise, ambition for expansion, and willingness to accept change, could always be accelerated to any extent required by policies which in themselves made profits easier and change less necessary.

From the late fifties, some economists had argued strongly that the real weakness of economic management was the lack of variability of the exchange rate; and after the evident failure of the Maudling strategy in 1964 this view rapidly gained adherents amongst economic advisers.

There were several reasons for supposing that by 1967, and possibly for several years before, sterling was over-valued. The most obvious manifestation was the trend of Britain's export prices compared with her rivals. Such figures are not conclusive: the goods being compared could not be directly competing with each other — for in that case Britain would have lost her trade altogether. And if we are comparing the price trends of distinctive products, it is difficult to know how far the trend of British prices represents the behaviour of a supplier slowly pricing itself out of markets and how far it was a consequence of concentration on more remunerative products: low export prices and large volumes are not automatically good in themselves. But, in fact, there was no evidence to suggest that the U.K. was successfully establishing herself in premium product markets. A less obvious, but possibly more important, manifestation of over-valuation was on the supply side — the relative unprofitability of exporting. For many producers the export market was not only more risky but also less profitable than the home market, and the likely consequence was that, in investing, firms planned for less expansion of output and less selling effort in export markets, leading to a low growth of exports. (On the other hand, the high average rates of profit that were being earned by British industry in the early sixties imply that, if the export markets were unprofitable, the home market must have been very profitable indeed; and this makes it doubtful whether devaluation would have had the desired effect in the late fifties or early sixties when it was first advocated.) Again, though committed to more liberalized trade, the government did, in fact, intervene in various ways that were thought to bring savings to the balance-of-payments (for example, in aircraft procurement) that implied an exchange rate distinctly lower than $2.80. The disadvantages of seeking to balance the current account by such measures were twofold: by operating on a narrow instead of a broad front the 'exchange premium' had to be much higher; and by operating with conjectural calculations it was likely that the exchange-saving effects would be exaggerated because of failure to take full account of imports indirectly caused. Finally, in 1964 relief was sought by the imposition of a 15 per cent import surcharge on manufacturers — a one-sided measure operating on imports only.

Devaluation was resisted for several reasons. The stability of the pound seemed important to maintain the use of sterling as an international currency; and to accept devaluation seemed to accept that the U.K.'s inflation rate must exceed that of other countries. In the event sterling, after being defended by large official borrowing, was overwhelmed by speculation.

So the $2.80 parity was swept away, and in its aftermath questioning the desirability of devaluation became almost an irrational heresy, so widespread had the view spread previously that it was necessary. It was 'necessary' in the sense of inevitable, and probably 'necessary' in the sense of being one of the measures needed to correct the United Kingdom's international position. But by itself it was not a remedy, and all the other factors necessary for its success were not obviously present.

9 The troubles of the seventies

At times in the mid-sixties devaluation had been seen as the principal measure needed to permit the accelerated expansion of an economy that would then no longer have to be held in check by policies of internal deflation to deal with balance-of-payments crises. In the event many of the expectations of devaluation were disappointed. In the short run there was an agonizing wait until 1969 before it could be seen to have brought any relief at all. And in the longer run, the British economy moved, after a boom in 1972–74, into a period of slower growth, more rapid inflation, and higher unemployment than at any time since the 1930s, despite the fact that the 1967 devaluation was followed by an abandonment of the system of fixed exchange rates in 1971. World conditions following the oil crisis of 1973 played a considerable part in the British situation. But important, perhaps predominant, causes were continuations of developments within the U.K. economy — growing government expenditure, inflation, and the declining profitability of industry — whose roots were established before 1967 and, some would say, came from Keynesian management itself. This chapter is primarily a review of these matters.

The foreign exchanges

'Devaluation' as a policy in the 1930s had been an attractive alternative to 'deflation', because, at a stroke, it made exports and import substitutes more price-competitive. It substituted for the painful, and apparently unfair, process of forcing down money wages in the export-trades, a 'rise' in prices with more general effect. It was acceptable because of the pain of the alternative, and because it did not actually cause prices to rise given the rate at which the other forces were pushing them down. If devaluation had a logic in the 1960s, it was as a substitute for the pain of the process of reversing the internal inflation. Yet if the inflation was caused by forces that were not easily controlled by reducing demand, that is, the concern of unions with the level of money prices and with relative incomes and profits, it was difficult to see how devaluation was going to have its full potential effects which involved increasing the relative prices of tradeable goods and the incomes of their producers. The ideology of the Prices and Incomes Policies introduced in 1964 and the Prime Minister's promise that 'the pound in your pocket will not be devalued' had not prepared the country for these adjustments. And indeed, in the short run, the government tried to suppress the effects of devaluation, both by holding down as long as possible the price of import substitutes and condemning exporters for allowing their profit margins to rise.

Moreover, devaluation did not totally avoid the need for a deflationary policy. The situation in the 1960s differed from the 1930s in another respect. In the 1930s there was unemployed labour and capacity in the export trades. In 1967 there was full employment. For devaluation to be effective in restoring equilibrium in the balance-of-payments, it would be necessary to reduce the level of existing domestic demands for British goods to make the resources used in these goods available either to produce exports or import substitutes. This would require deflation: a curbing of government expenditure and a reduction in the disposable incomes of consumers. That this was necessary was clearly recognized by the government, and devaluation was accompanied by higher taxation.

Devaluation did not work as quickly as had been hoped, and in 1968 import deposits were introduced to hamper imports and obtain temporary loans of foreign currency; and disposable incomes were further reduced by taxation. That devaluation should have worked slowly is not surprising; the correction required a fairly substantial shift of resources both within and between firms. British manufactures were not simple commodities sold from stock. They were, in many cases, goods produced to order; and in most cases goods for which markets had to be sought. There was one further point: British goods were in many cases sold at prices quoted in sterling. Consequently, for many months deliveries were being made at pre-devaluation prices, even where the goods had previously been competitively priced; and indeed, payments in sterling were being received for goods sold on credit long before devaluation.

Eventually, in 1969, the trade balance was righted and moved into surplus. The correction in relative prices had had to be accompanied by a sequence of markedly deflationary budgets so that the balance was achieved at a level of internal demand that left distinctly more unemployment. Moreover the rate of increase in wages, held back for three years, began to accelerate to a higher level than ever before despite the apparently high level of unemployment. Subsequently, in 1971, the United Kingdom in company with the rest of the world moved into a regime of variable exchange rates and the currency was allowed to depreciate more gradually. In theory such gradual movements should have been able to keep the U.K. 'on course' without the need for the very large 'once-for-all' adjustment of the kind needed in 1967. Why then, and in what sense, did the U.K. move into a phase of new and more acute payments crises?

The first factor to operate was the allowing, and indeed promoting, by the Conservative Chancellor, Barber, of an over-rapid expansion of demand that reached the limits of productive capacity in many sectors before unemployment had fallen to the levels achieved in the 1950s and 1960s. The boom in the U.K. coincided with a worldwide boom that increased the demand for commodities and raised their prices more quickly than at any time since the Korean War — an increase aggravated by a successful cartel among the oil-producing states which quintupled oil prices between 1970 and 1974. Even if the oil-producing states had been prepared to spend all of their increased revenue immediately, countries like the U.K. would have had instantaneously to achieve a shift of resources into the production of exports and to accept, because of the adverse movement in the terms of trade, a reduction in living standards.

Entry into the E.E.C., decided on in 1971 and brought into operation between 1973 and 1978, had two types of effect. In so far as it reduced the barriers to trade, it opened up opportunities to exporters at the same time as it increased competition from imports. This need not have had an adverse balance-of-payments effect or involved any net cost, if it had been possible to transfer resources quickly enough into sectors in which the U.K. had a comparative advantage. The second type of effect was the payment of a levy — in the forms of direct contributions to the cost of E.E.C. operations, a transfer to the E.E.C. of the revenue obtained from duties on food imports from outside the E.E.C., and the cost of the switch from cheaper imports of foodstuffs from the outside world to dearer E.E.C. sources. In some years, high prices outside the E.E.C. eliminated this latter element, and in all years there were some benefits received. On balance, however, there must have been some net cost which, though not serious in itself, aggravated an already weak balance-of-payments. This is not the place to pass judgement on entry into the E.E.C. The benefits, if benefits there be, are essentially long term and do not yet belong to the province of history.

For the U.K. the increased price of oil was a problem in the mid-seventies, but one not expected to be long run, because of the quite fortuitous good fortune of the discovery of substantial oil reserves in the North Sea. The oil was not obtainable immediately or without very heavy investment, which itself required many imports but did justify the incurring of an unprecedentedly large balance-of-payments deficit for several years. There was, however, excessive optimism about the speed and cost with which the new resources could be developed, which led to over-much borrowing in too short a form and exposed the U.K. to a crisis of confidence by its creditors in late 1976.

Balance-of-payments crises were necessarily different in a regime of variable exchange rates. Essentially they took the form of periods of very rapid depreciation of the pound. Because of the lag in the adjustment of trade to currency depreciation, there was no automatic stabilizing effect in the short run, and because of the effect of exchange rates on import prices there was a fairly quick aggravation of inflation as perceived internally, which threatened to offset any tendency of the depreciation to make British exports more competitive.

It is tempting to see the U.K.'s balance-of-payments crises of the mid- and late 1970s as the nemesis of those optimistic economists who had thought in the mid-sixties that devaluation was a weapon that could be used to offset any rate of internal inflation; and of those who pandered to the illusion held by her work-force that they were entitled to and could be given protection against any effect of prices on their standard of living. It is tempting to see the forces that are exhibited in the foreign exchange markets as being those of common sense reaction overcoming the obduracy of governments' refusals to face facts. This is an optimistic view. It would be justified if currency movements were indeed the product of what popular demonology supposes them to be, the profit-maximizing calculations of cool speculators. It is equally possible that they were the product of the actions of treasurers of international companies; and of others who were best informed about what their colleagues were doing and most concerned to avoid losses by failing to follow what they believe to be the general trend. There was a special problem in the 1970s created by the presence of the short-run funds of the oil states. But it may be that the problem was more fundamental: that a world in which financial barriers were largely removed was as unstable as a country in which there was no central bank.

Long-term trends in public expenditure and taxation

By 1950 demobilization of the economy had allowed current expenditure on goods and services by the Public Authorities to fall to 15·5 per cent of G.D.P., compared with 22·7 per cent in 1946 — not much higher than the 13·4 per cent of 1938. That it was so little more than 1938 may be partly attributable to the fact that wages and salaries in the public sector had not kept in step with the private sector.

On a wider definition of expenditure, that is, including National Insurance benefits and the interest on the National Debt, the percentage in 1950 was about 28 per cent compared with 23 per cent in 1938. To this might be added capital formation amounting to 6 per cent of G.D.P., compared with 3·5 per cent in 1938: this increase reflected the increased scope of the sector because of nationalization, though it did also reflect the extensive post-war building programmes. These expenditures hardly increased in the 1950s; and even in 1965 the expenditure on current goods and services had increased to only 16·8 per cent (or with transfers to 29 per cent) although capital formation was higher at 7·8 per cent. Thereafter the increases became much more noticeable to 17·7 per cent (32 per cent with transfers) in 1970; and 21·4 per cent (38 per cent with transfers) in 1975, with capital formation of 8 ·5 per cent. (These proportions are rather less than those often cited in contemporary controversy, because G.D.P. has been taken at market prices. The proportions of 55 or 60 per cent often cited are grossly misleading if they are taken to imply that the 100 less 55 or 60 per cent was a measure of the proportion of the G.D.P. left in the control of persons and companies for consumption or capital formation.)

Table 9.1 Principal components of public authorities current expenditure as percentages of G.D.P.

	1948	1953	1964	1975
Military Defence	7 ·04	8 ·64	5 ·96	4 ·92
National Health Service	1 ·97	2 ·84	3 ·16	4 ·59
Education	2 ·13	2 ·14	2 ·82	4 ·79
Other	5 ·88	4 ·64	4 ·80	7 ·87

Table 9.2 Age composition of population (percentages)

Percentage of Total Population	1901	1931	1951	1971
Males of Working Age	30 ·1	32 ·7	32 ·4	31 ·2
Females of Working Age	31 ·1	33 ·8	31 ·6	28 ·3
All under Working Age	32 ·5	24 ·2	22 ·5	24 ·1
All over Working Age	6 ·3	9 ·3	13 ·6	16 ·3

The main component factors of the explosive increase after 1965, education, the Health Service, and pensions and grants, had been increasing in relative importance before 1965. But increases until then were masked by the possibility of making very considerable cuts in defence expenditure (beginning in 1954) and, very much less important, by the fact that inflation was offsetting increased interest rates and reducing the real cost of interest payments (even though the debt was increasing). Two types of factor account for the increase in real expenditure. First, demography: the rapidly increasing proportion of old people in the population, requiring pensions and making greater demands on health and welfare services; and the need to educate a larger population of children consequent on the higher birth rate of post-war years. Second, changing standards of provision, the most obvious examples being extension of higher education, and the reduction of pupil/teacher ratios. In some cases a decision can be identified which started the processes, but in practice the actual decisions may have taken many years before they stopped adding to expenditure; it takes time to increase the number of university places, and, because professional people are paid on scales which will rise with age, it may take even longer before the financial cost stops rising. Some part of the increase between 1970 and 1975 is to be explained in this way; but it was also the case that standards of provision, particularly of social benefits, were increased further in these years, and the greater numbers of unemployed increased needs as well. Throughout the period until 1970, the cost to the community of the public sector was increased by a fairly steady one per cent per annum increase in the 'price' of its services relative to those of the rest of the economy — reflecting the concentration of productivity growth (or at least measurable growth) in the private sector. After 1970 the trend accelerated, reflecting an increase in wages and salaries in the public sector relative to the private sector.

Expenditures on education, health, and welfare benefits were very much the most important categories of expenditure. But expenditure on the Police Force rose in money terms (from £57 million to £905 million) between 1950 and 1975 by a multiple (15·9 times) that is less than the multiple for education (19 times) but distinctly more than for the National Health Service (12 times). This increase no doubt reflects the heavy demands of traffic control as well as the cost of replacing bicycles with cars and sophisticated equipment. Expenditure on the Fire Service also rose by the same proportion — reflecting both a rise in labour costs in a labour-intensive service and the need for improved equipment to deal with greater industrial hazards. Expenditure on Libraries and Museums also increased by a very similar proportion.

The worthwhileness of these expenditures was a matter of controversy between those who passionately believed in their social benefits and those who doubted whether the prospective benefits were properly weighed against the full costs. It is less controversial that the rate of growth of expenditure, particularly between 1970 and 1975, was not fully anticipated, and contributed to the economic problems of the period.

Government forecasting was usually done in 'real' rather than 'money' terms, in order to make one year comparable with another. This made a systematic difference because of the change in relative prices between the public and private sector: when measured in real terms, public expenditure on goods and services as a percentage of G.D.P. actually fell from 21·9 per cent in 1950 to 19·2 per cent in 1975, although in money terms it had risen from 15·5 per cent to 21·4 per cent. The 'real' approach led to neglect of the fact that the extent to which taxes or borrowings would have to increase was determined by the proportionate importance of public expenditure in money terms. Indeed, planning in real terms had been introduced as a significant reform on the recommendation of Lord Plowden in 1961, in a reform that had also encouraged the planners of public expenditure to build an assumed rate of growth of G.D.P. into their plans. The effect of this was aggravated by the fact that it took over from N.E.D.C. the very optimistic assumption that real growth would be possible at a rate of 4 per cent p.a. — a rate increased to 4½ per cent by the Labour Government in 1965. Considering matters in real terms may also have led to concentration on the public sector's demand for real resources, paying less attention to its transfer commitments; regarding them, that is, pensions and grants, as effectively simple transfers between one part of the personal sector and another. It is true that, looked at from the point of view of the country as a whole, the support of the old by the working population is not fundamentally different from the support of children. Nevertheless, in the former case the transfer has to be made via the taxation system (and adds to the 'burden of taxation') while in the second case the costs of maintenance are usually made within the family, constituting a burden for parents but having no fiscal effects.

It must also be doubted whether those responsible for the original decisions that led to expenditures had been aware of the full extent of their eventual likely size. An important factor was the system of delegation of financial responsibility within the public sector from central to local government. If the two are separated, we find that the growth in local government current expenditure was continuous after 1950 — again showing acceleration, but throughout the whole twenty-five years. The responsibility of local authorities for education does not explain this; for if education is taken out the increase is almost the same until 1970, though it explains a large part of the acceleration thereafter. Much of the increase of expenditure reflected national government policy, and was promoted by grants. But it also seems likely that local authorities were led both into rapid expansion and into some laxity of control by a phase of relative financial ease caused by the buoyancy of rate revenue from the 're-rating' of industry in 1963 and from the redevelopment of city centres. The grant system itself could also lead to uncritical commitments simply because the money was there.

With the important exception of schools and hospitals, the main items constituting 'Public Capital Formation' are not related to the largest current expenditures of the public sector. They were either the expenditures on plant and equipment of the nationalized industries or the expenditure on housing of the local authorities and new towns, or the expenditure on roads of the central and local government. The reason for considering them together is that the expenditures were largely financed by borrowing. In the case of the nationalized industries, this borrowing was largely from the central government which had in turn to finance the lending. Local authorities had the power to go to the long-term capital market and also, after 1957, financed a great deal of their debt by short-term borrowing; in doing so they were largely competing with the central government for funds. Over the whole period, Gross Fixed Capital Formation by the public sector grew from 6·0 per cent to 8·2 per cent, but this was not a steady growth, nor did it comprise smoothly growing components. In the early fifties the large items were local authority housing and power stations. In the second half of the fifties, railways. In the 1960s electricity was run down, then sharply increased. The road programme accelerated and telecommunications expanded to become one of the largest of all items.

Outside the nationalized industries public capital spending tended to be dominated by administrative factors. Since authorization of projects was not related to any economic assessment of the returns, and since the authorities concerned had no opportunity to choose between capital and current expenditures there was virtually no incentive to seek to keep down running costs. Indeed there was a tendency to seek as high a standard of construction as would be allowed, and subsequently to regard this as an entitlement to the current expenditure necessary to make full use of the building.

We have perhaps considered these matters too much in circumstantial detail. At least part of the problem with public expenditure in the 1970s arose out of the Keynesian revolution of the 1940s. If, to control the overall level of activity in the economy, the raising of revenue and the commitment to expenditure were no longer to be associated as they had been under orthodox systems of balancing the budget, the traditional disciplines on expenditure were removed, because the worthwhileness of expenditive proposals had no longer to be assessed against their implications for taxation. Moreover, there were further problems, because very little public expenditure was suitable for year to year variation on Keynesian principles. (The time-honoured notion of giving the unemployed shovels to build roads had itself ceased to be feasible). In fact, a good many public expenditure projects involved greater commitments in the further, than in the near, future. There was thus, from time to time, a situation in which the government found 'room' in the current state of the economy for extra expenditure; and accepted expenditure proposals, often hurriedly (because of the need to create employment) and consequently without considering their full future implications (which in any case the groups pressing for the expenditures were likely to conceal). Thus, largely without intention, the fiscal burden crept upwards — a growth made easier by the natural tendency of direct taxation to expand more quickly than G.N.P.

However, the wastes that accompanied the expansion of public expediture should not completely distract us from fundamental factors underlying growth in public expenditure: a change in relative costs because of lower productivity-growth in the public sector; and a genuine desire, or need, for more services of the type provided by public expenditure. In such a society economic growth will almost inevitably cause the relative importance of public expenditure to increase. The levels of public expenditure reached in the U.K. in relation to G.D.P. were high, but not uniquely high, by international standards. What was distinct about the British case was that the high proportion was reached at a much lower average income than was the case of most other developed countries, and this entailed higher rates of taxation at lower incomes than elsewhere.

Table 9.3 Composition of taxation (central and local)

Form of Tax	1948	1955	1960	1965	1970	1975
Capital	5·0	3·2	3·2	2·6	3·5	2·2
Expenditure	49·4	46·4	46·7	45·3	43·9	37·1
Wage & Salaries	10·3	11·9	15·6	17·9	20·6	30·0
Employees National Insurance	3·9	4·9	6·0	7·2	6·2	6·8
Other Direct including Employers N.I.	31·2	33·6	28·4	27·0	25·8	23·9

In the long run there was a distinct increase in reliance on direct taxes (i.e. taxes on income) in contrast to indirect taxes. In 1948, 45 per cent of government revenue was obtained from direct taxation and a further 9 per cent from National Insurance contributions (which at that time were not graduated and were, effectively, a poll tax on employment). By 1975 the proportion of direct taxes themselves was 49 per cent but National Insurance contributions (now proportional to income) were 21 per cent of central government revenue. The main part of the change is explicable in terms of political acceptability. Increasing indirect taxes involved, where they were stated in money terms, specific action which attracted unfavourable notice, especially in a period of inflation; other indirect taxes increased automatically but then only in proportion to income. By contrast, the system by which tax-free allowances were given against income produced a tendency for direct taxation revenue to rise more than in proportion to incomes, and this happened whether the growth in incomes was real or in money terms, except in so far as the size of the allowances was specifically revised in response to inflation. This phenomenon of 'fiscal drag' when first noticed by economists was regarded with favour as 'an automatic stabilizer'; but in times of more rapid inflation 'fiscal drag' became a term of abuse when perceived by a wider audience.

The incidence of the increase in direct taxation was not even. In 1948 income tax on wages and salaries constituted a quarter of the revenue from direct taxes, in 1975 it constituted 60 per cent. This change in proportionate contribution reflects the declining importance of company taxation, in part because of the falling share of profits in national income and in part because of the policy of providing extensive investment incentives by the remission of taxation. And, indeed, the need in 1974 to make allowance for the finance of stocks virtually suspended the taxing of companies' profits, except in so far as they were distributed as dividends, and contributed to the extent of the public deficit at that time. Nor within the category of wages and salaries was the increase in incidence even. Apart from effectively re-imposing rates of tax on high incomes at their wartime level, there was little scope for increasing tax rates on the top-most ranges of income. Thus altogether between 1959 and 1974–5, the percentage of their incomes paid in direct tax by the top 10 per cent of income earners increased from 23·5 per cent to 29·1 per cent, but their share of the total direct tax paid by individuals fell from 65 per cent to 42 per cent.

The main way to increase tax revenue had to be by allowing the lower limit of the taxation range to fall. In 1938 the full rate of income tax was not payable until an annual income (in 1970 pounds) of £2,206 was received, and above this level tax led to a deduction of less than a quarter of additional income; some tax at a lower rate was paid at incomes above £1,521. But even this level of income was *twice* the average earnings of manual labour, and greater than the earnings of many non-manual workers. Tax revenue was obtained in wartime by increasing rates of tax and leaving allowances uncorrected for wartime inflation (with the exception of a wife's earned income allowance). The effect was that in 1948 a manual worker with average earnings would just be paying tax, though only at a rate of 12 per cent; he had to have nearly twice as much to reach the standard rate of 36 per cent. In the next decade the thresholds were maintained in real terms, though the rise in average earnings slightly reduced their relative position; on the other hand the highest rate of tax was reduced to about 30 per cent.

Three elements contributed to the dramatic change of the next fifteen years: intermediate rates of tax were abolished in the 1969 budget; the tax rate above this threshold was 33 per cent; and it is arguable that the employees' contribution to National Insurance, which from 1975 were proportionate to income, should be added to this. The threshold for income tax was little more than half the average manual earnings (and was sometimes below the level at which social security payments were obtainable); in real terms it was 60 per cent of the lower 1938 threshold and less than half the threshold at which the standard rate had been paid.

That the tax threshold should have fallen in relation to real earnings was a natural consequence of the redistribution of income in favour of the manual wage-earner; that it should have fallen absolutely was a simple consequence of the greater proportionate importance of government expenditure. Much of this expenditure was, of course, of benefit to individual workers and was sometimes termed the social wage; but clearly for every individual it constituted a charge on extra earnings, the amount of which bore no directly visible relation to the benefits derived.

Inflation

Between 1935 and 1975 prices in the U.K. rose eightfold. This rate of inflation was trivial by the standards of some other countries, where hyperinflations have led to the complete collapse of currencies within short periods; and quite low by comparison with the rates sustained for long periods in many Latin-American countries. It was, however, quite unprecedented in British history — the previous eightfold increase had taken four centuries rather than four decades.

Table 9.4 Price and earnings multiples

Factor by which multiplied	1935/45	45/55	between 55/65	65/75	Total Multiplication
Houses	2·34	1·68	1·25	2·74	13·5
All Capital Goods	2·10	1·73	1·26	2·51	11·5
All Consumer Goods and Services	1·70	1·54	1·34	2·25	7·9
Male Earnings	1·88	1·84	1·76	3·04	18·5
Female Earnings	2·02	1·83	1·66	3·56	21·8

Price increases for different classes of goods varied considerably around the overall average, with the prices of consumer goods generally increasing less than the prices of capital goods — particularly of houses (where the thirteenfold increase is for the building only and excludes the effect of the changing price of land). These differences primarily reflect differences in the extent to which growth in productivity offset the growth of labour costs that underlay the rise in prices. If individual goods had been considered, even more striking contrasts would have been found; with goods where labour productivity had been enhanced by innovation and economies of scale at one end of the spectrum, and cases at the other end where there had been very little technical change and the rise in labour costs, because it took no account of the reduced length of the working year (for example, stone masonry repairs).

The inflation in 1935–75 was not unique to the United Kingdom. Particularly in the War and immediate post-war period, say 1939–53, and again towards the end of the period — perhaps beginning in 1967 but concentrated mainly in the 1970's — there was a considerable rise in import prices. This primarily reflected a rise in the price of foodstuffs and raw materials outside the U.K. though it was also affected by the depreciation of the pound sterling — a depreciation which itself may be thought of as a rough indication of the excess inflation in the U.K. as compared with the U.S.A. during the whole period. In 1939–53 the U.K.'s inflation was, by international standards, small; for almost all currencies depreciated against the dollar. Between 1953 and 1967 inflation in the U.K. was only slightly faster than in other countries, though the difference in the growth of export prices was greater than the difference in internal price levels, suggesting that the difference was primarily associated with different rates of productivity growth in manufacturing industry.

Inspection of Figure 9·1 shows that the same three phases 1939–53, 1953–67 and 1967–75 had very different rates of inflation, with inflation in the middle period never exceeding 5 per cent a year and averaging distinctly less. It would be wrong, however, to assume that in all senses inflation abated in the middle period. Until the early fifties inflation could be regarded as an abnormality; wars had usually been associated with sharp increases in prices. What the next fifteen years were to show was that inflation, though

Figure 9.1 Inflation (percentage increases over previous year)

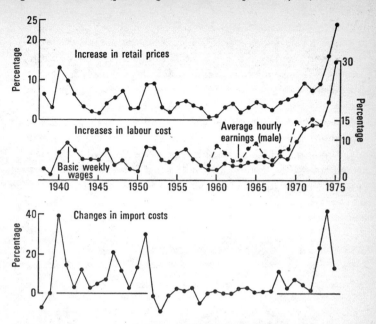

it had diminished, had not vanished. It was in that period that institutions and expectations were adapted to a continuation of inflation that laid a foundation for the explosive inflation of the 1970s.

Such expectations were embodied in various institutional changes. It came to be expected by employer and employee that revisions of wage and salary contracts should be made frequently (by 1967 this was, in most cases, annually). Commercial rents that traditionally had been fixed for twenty-one years or even longer were, in leases made in the 1960s, generally reviewable after seven years. Trust law was revised to enable trustees to invest in ordinary shares, which were thought to be assets that had more chance of preserving their value in inflation. More generally, wealth-owning individuals and institutions showed an increasing consciousness of the merits of real assets, equities, and property, as opposed to loans repayable in money. This was reflected in the 'reverse yield gap', the excess of current yield expected from bonds as compared with equities, which appeared about 1960. More widely, it was a contributory factor to the boom in owner occupation — and indeed to the general mania for collecting objects that were thought to have realizable value. With such manifestations went a general alertness to the dangers of inflation: an alertness that would itself contribute to the acceleration of inflation in the 1970s.

During the War there was considerable concern to keep down the pace of inflation, presumably from fears of the development of hyperinflation seen in other wartime and post-war economies. In the immediate post-war period, although some economists saw wage-inflation as a great problem in a world of full employment, the Labour Government did not, possibly because of the firm opposition of Ernest Bevin, attempt to do more than persuade the unions to restrain wage demands in the short run. The subsequent Conservative Government was, perhaps, even more unwilling to erect and maintain policies to control the rise in wages because of its concern not to seem anti-union.

In the early 1960s concern was expressed about inflation and some steps taken to deal with it: the Council on Productivity, Prices, and Incomes of 1957 was succeeded by the National Incomes Commission of 1962 and the National Board for Prices and Incomes (N.B.P.I.) of 1965. A short wage freeze was introduced in 1961; a longer term policy of control accompanied the N.B.P.I. in 1965; and this was tightened to a complete standstill in July 1966. Despite these measures, determination to deal with inflation was less than whole-hearted because the necessity of doing so was not universally agreed. Its main disadvantage was seen in relation to export pricing, and many were tempted to think that with a different policy towards the currency parity it would be no problem at all — failing to recognize that devaluation itself would tend to increase the forces that contributed to inflation and that its effectiveness could be nullified by further inflation. The actual rate of inflation had been low and sustained for a long period and this tended to dissipate fears of acceleration. The fact that institutionally the economy was much more educated to inflation was ignored. On the other hand, excessive weight was given to the 'Phillips Curve', a relationship between prices and employment for a long period during which inflation had never been expected. The Phillips curve was capable of two interpretations: either that for a quite low rate of inflation a high level of employment could be purchased; or that, if necessary, it would always be possible for the managers of the economy to turn off inflation by producing some increase of unemployment. Some economists even thought a low rate of inflation of positive advantage; the harm done was seen primarily in its effect in making export prices uncompetitive; lip-service was paid to its distributional effects; and virtually no attention at all was paid to the possibility that it was producing wasteful distortions in investment.

Towards the end of the Labour Government in 1970, when devaluation seemed to be working, wages were allowed to rise more rapidly, and on its accession the Conservative government abolished the N.B.P.I. Despite relatively high unemployment, wages now rose more quickly than they had ever done — destroying the simple Phillips Curve relationship. By 1971 the Confederation of British Industries organized voluntary price restraint. In 1972 official prices and incomes policies were resumed. This policy was broken by the miners' strike of 1974 and the electoral defeat of the Conservatives. The Wilson government suspended the attempt to restrain wages until August 1975, while retaining the Price Commission in being; but then felt compelled to resume the attempt to curb incomes.

In considering the complex history of incomes policies over a period of almost twenty years, there is a temptation to simplify by talking the language of economic management, as though incomes policies were valves to be turned 'on' and 'off'. In fact each episode had its own distinctive characteristics. The Heath policies of 1972–4, for example, endeavoured, in the detailed form of their prices policies, to put pressure on firms to resist wage demands; on the other hand, the ceilings set for the direct control of wages depended for their success on the maintenance of the growth of real income experienced in the upsurging of the Barber boom, and were vulnerable to the risk of a rise in import prices. More important, each episode generated experience and expectations which remained. Thus unions became increasingly conscious of the need to force a catching-up on their ambitions before the next period of freeze occurred; and the form of the policies, for example, setting national norms or allowing for productivity increases, may themselves have helped as much to form national opinion about the ethics of income distribution as to express it.

In the period 1945–51, and again in 1972–4, some noticeable part of the rise in the U.K. price level could be directly ascribed to the rise in the world market prices of imported foodstuffs or materials for which there are no domestic substitutes. But we need to be careful about the interpretation we place on the sequence of events. The rise in import prices accounted directly for some of the rise in the price level. The further indirect effect of import prices via increases in money wages intended to 'compensate' for the rise in prices was really attributable to the institutional arrangements that produced the increase in money incomes, and to the economic power that had enforced them. In periods other than those mentioned, increases in world prices made no contribution to U.K. prices.

There is only one important case, house building, where the rise in prices was visibly directly associated with the excess demand for goods themselves. In most cases inflation seemed primarily to take the form of increasing labour costs, leading manufacturers to increase prices. We must recognize that appearances might be deceptive and that the impression might be part of manufacturers' public relations with their customers, but it would seem to have confirmation in the fact that the greatest price increases occurred not in the upswing and boom of the cycle when demand was growing most rapidly but after the downturn when increasing outlays on wages could not be spread over larger output. It does not seem, therefore, that inflation was directly associated with excess demand for goods.

The important question is, then, how far the inflation in the United Kingdom, which was undoubtedly primarily associated with an increase in labour costs, was itself associated with a high level of demand for labour (and, by implication, how far it would have been reduced by acceptance of higher levels of unemployment). In the process of wage-negotiation, claims were put forward and discussed on grounds of cost of living increases, increased wages in comparable occupations, productivity increases, and the profitability of the employing firms. In one extreme view, all this was superficial and disguised the operation of simpler, more basic, forces of supply and demand. In this view, the outcome of negotiations was primarily determined by the 'real' bargaining power of the two sides, the balance of which was affected by the general level of demand; the higher the level of demand, the more employers had to lose from a strike in lost sales, and the more easily employees could find other jobs to support them temporarily. The view seemed particularly appropriate to the case of some industries, especially the important engineering industry, where an additional factor operated. Local bargains that were very much more directly concerned with attracting and retaining labour and persuading it to accept new assignments were very important modifiers of what had been agreed nationally, and were fairly clearly sensitive to the pressure of demand for their products felt by the employers.

The latter point is plausible as a significant contributor to the inflationary process in engineering in the fifties and sixties, in building wages, and possibly in other sectors. Excess demand for output and shortages of labour induced a process of 'bidding' which pushed up earnings. And no doubt the effects, particuarly on the building industry, which was a potential employment for many workers in other sectors, might be diffused as employees in these other sectors contrived to increase their wages too. It is difficult, however, to see this as a complete explanation for the 1970s. It may well be that despite the rise in general unemployment there continued to be a shortage of skilled labour. And it certainly was the case in the Barber boom that simple demand pushed up the rates obtainable by self-employed building workers. But it was, nevertheless, a period in which wages in the public sector, more visibly related to strikes and industrial discontent than to shortage of labour, no longer followed the private sector. Though in the case of the miners, a free market might have given a large increase in wages because of the effect of the increased price of oil on the value of their marginal product, their actual increases were won by determined industrial action.

The proposition that the outcome of all formal bargaining merely disguises the effect of supply and demand is implausible. As argued earlier, unions, particularly in the short run, had a great deal of monopoly power. The extent to which they used this power is not entirely to be explained by the extent of the current demand for their services. Thus, for example, claims based on cost of living increases, or comparability with other workers, will create potential support and enthusiasm for a strike that are not correlated with the current level of demand. Nor do these factors work only where strong unions exist. Many firms depend on the willing co-operation of at least some of their workers in showing initiative, effort, and loyalty, and these qualities may be damaged unless the firm in revising wages and salaries pays heed to these socially approved principles and does not seem to be changing course at every variation of pressure in the labour market.

The argument being put forward is that union coercive power supplemented by the occurrence of periods of excess demand for labour made more important principles like 'cost of living compensation', 'comparability', and 'productivity reward', which acquired a life of their own. But other factors contributed to these principles. Incomes policy legitimized the idea that there was a national minimum increase to which everyone was entitled. Publicity was given to productivity and created the impression that workers always had a right to share directly in the benefits of increased productivity.

None of the principles is unreasonable, and none, taken individually, need cause an inflation, but taken together they could easily do so. If the workers in occupations where productivity improves get corresponding increases in wages, and other groups match them on principle of comparability, there must be an inflation, the pace of which will be accelerated the more 'cost of living' is invoked as an addition to the other justifications for a wage increase. In emphasizing the importance of the operation of such principles, it is not being suggested that they operated without modification. Taken in that sense they would have produced a much more explosive inflation than did actually occur. It is clear that, in the event, most groups of income earners at most times had to accept lower real incomes than the full application of all principles would have entitled them to.

Acknowledging this latter point is not, however, to accept the pure monetarist position, that is, the notion that, whatever the state of feeling about the justice of wage claims, wage increases could have been limited by a sufficiently determined restriction of the money supply. A tighter monetary policy in the early seventies would have done something to abate the pressure of demand; how far it would have led to a more determined resistance to wage claims is far from clear. It is probably the case that, in 1974–5, monetary tightness was limiting the extent to which wages were allowed to rise in the private sector; but it depended on a situation in which a very large part of industry was faced with bankruptcy— not a state of affairs that could be accepted as part of a normal mechanism of control. Success in controlling monetary expansion was a useful measure of the success of policies controlling inflation, but it was quite wrong to suppose that an economy with a large public sector and with many financially weak large firms could be controlled in the way the Bank of England had controlled the pre-1914 economy.

On one type of explanation — that which emphasizes the determination of labour unions to maintain relativities — increasing productivity and increasing real incomes did nothing to reduce inflation. Indeed, in so far as the increase in productivity was concentrated in particular sectors and incomes were increased in those sectors in step with the productivity increases, inflation was exacerbated. An alternative explanation would see inflation as provoked by a failure of real incomes to rise. It is plausible that, had British Governments after 1960 not increased public expenditure and taxation as rapidly as they did, so that the personal disposable incomes of labour had risen more quickly, there would have been less inflation; and there was a certain amount of evidence that in calculating wage increases necessary to maintain standards, unions took account of the high rates of taxation incurred by their members on any increase in their money income. Such an explanation does not, however, take account of the very large increases in real incomes of wage-earners that did occur in the early seventies.

Unemployment: the regional problem

A notorious aspect of inter-war unemployment was its concentration in particular regions — South Wales, Scotland, Lancashire, West Cumberland, and the North East — associated with coal production (especially for export, but also the marginal producers), cotton production, and shipbuilding. During the War the unemployment disappeared, partly because of the revival of shipbuilding and heavy engineering, partly because War contracts were steered to wherever labour was available, and partly because conscription removed a large part of the labour supply.

At the end of the War measures that had already been taken in the 1930s to develop industrial estates in the Special Areas were extended by the use of building licenses and the requirements under the Town and Country Planning Act that developments should be certified as conforming to location policy for the redesignated Development Areas. In fact, though some new industries were steered to these areas immediately after the War, the powerful weapon of prohibiting development outside the Development Areas fell into disuse in the early 1950s. At that stage, with excess demand for coal and a long order book for shipping, and with the favourable effects of industry already attracted, the problem of the regions seemed largely solved.

In the later 1950s, as new investment began to displace older factories, marginal mines began to close, and the longer order book of the shipbuilders was worked off, there was renewed consciousness of the problem; financial assistance was extended to new Development Districts, pressure was put on the car industry to expand its capacity by new plants in Scotland and on Merseyside, a new integrated steelworks project was divided between Wales and Scotland, and there was some revival in the use of Industrial Development Certificates to prohibit development elsewhere. However, though these measures in themselves must have had considerable effect, the problems precipitating the unemployment, in particular the decline of shipbuilding and coal mining, grew. Further steps were taken in the 1960s to make available to all firms in the Development Areas fiscal investment incentives — in addition to the grants available for certain new projects: subsequently a subsidy for all employment (the Regional Employment Premium) was added, and a category of areas with very acute problems (the Special Development Areas) introduced. At the same time, despite the increase in the positive incentives, the power to prohibit development elsewhere was much more frequently used. Some attempt was also made under the Office Development Act 1964 to restrict the growth of office employment in Central London.

There was no doubt that the Development Areas had problems because of their high levels of unemployment and, in an age concerned to shield citizens from exceptional hardship, there was a case for employment creating projects in the Development Areas. But the questions must be asked why attention was concentrated so exclusively on taking work to the workers, whether the total sums used were disproportionate to the need, and whether there was not a danger of detracting from the general efficiency of industry in trying to solve such an acute problem in so short a time by dependence on prohibitory powers.

It was argued that a regional policy might, in addition to its social benefits, have net economic advantage. Businesses could be ignorant (and possibly prejudiced in seeking to expand where they had always been); the costs of providing social capital in already congested areas were not taken into account; and if capacity could be increased in the Development Areas it would be possible to run the economy at a higher level of demand. All these arguments were plausible: the difficulty was in establishing what they would imply administratively. As it was they tended to be used to justify an extreme policy in which the development areas were not only helped by regional policy, but their industries like shipbuilding were directly subsidized and given cheap credit, and more generous criteria were applied in judging their need for roads and other social capital. Perhaps most serious was the damage to industrial development elsewhere, either by the enforcement of split operations (which though feasible at one point in time might involve exceptional problems for management and damage firms future operations) and sub-optimal sized plants, or simply from its deterrence to investment. This is an example of a general problem in economic policy: economic reasoning would suggest a limited amount of intervention, but without a very clear statement of how in fact that limit is to be determined the policy could be pushed much too far.

Unemployment: the national problem

Until 1965 there was little sign of long-term general unemployment. After 1955, recessions had been a little deeper and in boom periods unemployment remained over 300,000, but this was little more than a reflection of the growing structural unemployment of the regions. After 1966 there was a more distinct worsening:

unemployment hovered around 600,000 until 1970, touched 950,000 before the Barber boom 1972–4, in which it never fell below 500,000. There was then a more rapid deterioration to over a million by the end of 1975 and almost a million and a half in 1977 — despite various types of measure designed to reduce registered unemployment. It needs to be considered how far this failure to maintain full employment can be explained in the terms of economic management and how far it was the consequence of factors which the simplified Keynesian orthodoxy of the post-war period obscured.

As figure 8·1 shows, the variation in unemployment was distinctly less than the variation of G.D.P. about its average growth rate. This divergence in the proportionate size of fluctuations was greater than it had been in the inter-war period. It was a consequence both of long-run technical changes and changed relations with the work-force. Increased mechanization tended to reduce the amount of 'direct' labour used without a corresponding increase in the amount of overhead labour, and also had the effect that certain types of production required a large minimum complement, for example, to man the stations of an assembly line or to monitor the controls of a process plant. Expectations of a high long-run demand for labour made firms unwilling to lay-off labour, especially skilled labour, in recessions they believed temporary, so they hoarded labour. And more formally unions resisted lay-offs and tried to persuade managers to share work. It has been conjectured that hoarding was important until 1966, when there was a 'shake-out' caused by a revision of expectations about the normality of a shortage of labour. On the other hand, the introduction of laws providing substantial compensation for redundancy, and requiring several months notice, perhaps offset this and continued partially to insulate the level of employment from short-term fluctuations in the level of output.

The fact that employment of labour was less easy to vary with output in the short run had two related consequences. First, its direct counterpart was that for a given variation in volume of sales the variation of profits was greater than it would have been if labour had been a more variable cost; a fall in sales volume was more likely to push a plant into a situation in which it made losses, and to compel the firm owning the plant to think of the advantages and disadvantages of its permanent closure. Secondly, because giving employment became more of a permanent commitment, it became one that employers were more cautious about entering into; although this may be difficult to distinguish from other elements that simply increased the cost of labour.

This raises the fundamental question. The Keynesian model sees a demand for goods and services being fairly automatically translated into a demand for labour. This is not an implausible picture of short-run fluctuations with periods of recession, in which there are unemployed factories waiting for men to return to them when demand revives. But it seems incomplete in the long run for an economy experiencing growth and technical change. For in such a case the maintenance of full employment requires that the growth of the available labour-force should match the net rate at which employment opportunities are being created; this net rate being the difference between the jobs available in new factories and the rate at which jobs are lost because of the permanent closure of factories which for one reason or another have become uneconomic. This net rate will not be insensitive to levels of demand for output — high levels of demand will keep old factories open for longer than otherwise and may improve investment prospects; but demand in itself is insufficient to ensure profitability.

Figure 9·2 Civil employment 1920–75

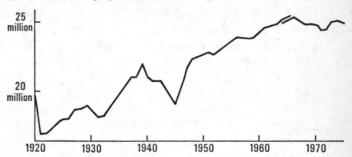

This suggests that we should look at employment as well as unemployment. The picture of employment is quite remarkable. For eighteen years until 1966 civil employment growth was about ¾ per cent per year and closely followed a path that was not far from a projection of the inter-war trend, and not very much lower than the 0·88 per cent growth of the period 1855–1920. Such growth could not have continued indefinitely, since it was much faster than the growth of the population of working age and was dependent on the extended participation of women. We should therefore have expected a levelling off, especially since the age-distribution of the labour-force was due to produce a large number of retirements from about the mid-sixties. On the other hand, we would have expected that such levelling off would have been accompanied by symptoms of *increased* labour-shortage, that is, lower unemployment and higher vacancies; and we would have expected the growth of employment gradually to decelerate. (Such labour shortages were indeed anticipated in the National Plan of 1965.) But what we actually find is not only an abrupt end to growth but an actual *reversal*, with no signs of general tightness in the labour market. It seems clear that, for some reason or another, there was an abrupt change in the growth of demand for labour about the mid-sixties.

Employment in manufacturing shows a slightly different picture; although generally it showed more fluctuations than total employment, its underlying trend shows a less abrupt change of direction in 1966 — raising the question whether the initial slackening in the growth of demand for labour had been disguised by the boom of the early sixties. Caution is required here. Some would question whether the labour market after 1966 did display greater general slack. It has been contended that the higher level of unemployment was due to the introduction of more generous redundancy payments, and of levels of unemployment pay which were related to previous earnings; both of which enabled the unemployed to take longer in searching for their next job. It is also pointed out that unfilled vacancies remained high, and were as high in 1973 as they had been in earlier booms. Nevertheless, even if these points are admitted, and the first is very disputable, they do not make much difference to the picture given by the employment graph itself of an end, perhaps an abrupt end, to the growth of demand for labour.

The turning-point in the labour market in the mid-1960s may in part have been a delayed response to changes in labour costs and technical change that had already occurred several years before, but which had been tolerated by management in a period of high profits. Now with profit rates falling, liquid reserves depleted, and in many cases with firms taken-over by more profit-conscious managers, began a period in which the unprofitable factories were weeded out. The size of labour costs was not simply a matter of wage rates. National Insurance, and, outside industry, Selective Employment Tax (S.E.T.), added significantly to *per capita* labour costs. The replacement of S.E.T. by a graduated system of National Insurance in 1973, and subsequent increases in the rates of National Insurance, extended the cost to all sectors. Legislation providing substantial payments in case of redundancy (1965), and, as in fact operated, almost universal compensation for dismissal, combined to make the offer of employment a more permanent commitment than it had been, the relevant cost of which was not the current wage but the uncertain obligations acquired for the future.

Put in more general terms this type of explanation seems to be suggesting that labour had become overpriced, either in the sense that it had led to businessmen selecting production recipes that were too labour-saving to create enough new jobs and to closure of factories, or in the sense that it had curtailed the flow of funds for investment. A Keynesian would question this by suggesting that both factors would have been diminished by higher levels of demand. But high levels of demand while *necessary* may not be *sufficient* to stimulate enough investment — especially where high levels of demand were expected to accelerate the rise in wage costs and where the ability to increase prices was limited by international competition.

Direct information about profitability for the early part of the period is rather fragmentary, and for the whole period is made difficult to interpret, because accounts made inadequate provision for inflation. The real rate of profit before tax in private sector companies was probably well over 10 per cent in the 1950s possibly very much the same as it had been in the late thirties. Within the period 1948–64, it may have shown some tendency to rise until 1955, and then start falling away again, but the evidence for these changes is hazy before 1960. Chart 9.3 presents the much more reliable data available for the period after 1960. It presents a picture of the rate of profit drooping in the sixties and collapsing in the mid-seventies. During the whole period the profit on manufacturing was consistently below the general level in the economy as a whole as shown on the chart. After tax, the fall in the 1960s was greater in proportionate terms (much more than halved), the operation of investment incentives being offset by the taxing of increases in the value of stocks. Without the emergency stock relief introduced in 1974 (dashed line in Chart 9.3) profits would have disappeared altogether in 1974.

Figure 9.3 Return on capital 1960–74

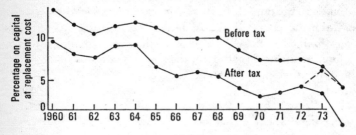

Note: The after-tax rate excludes the effects of stock relief which was introduced in 1974. The dashed line after 1972 shows the effects of this relief.
Source: J. S. Flemming: 'Rate of Return on Capital Employed by Commercial and Industrial Companies 1960–74' in *Bank of England Bulletin*, March 1976.

One explanation for the fall is in terms of labour bargaining power — the collective ability of the work-force to obtain a larger share of the net product of firms. This theory requires the operation of some sort of factor which leads firms not to pass on the increase in their wage costs to an extent sufficient to maintain their profit margins. The most obvious case of this was under the voluntary price-freeze followed by the operation of the Price Commission in the 1970s, or the effect of the operation of the Prices and Incomes Board in the 1960s. Another type of limit was produced by foreign competition, particularly in the period before the 1967 devaluation. There are two types of limit to labour's bargaining power: faced with lower profitability, managers may reduce the rate at which they invest and add to the capital stock, and thus face labour with the prospect of gradually increasing unemployment; or, in more extreme conditions where they are faced with more acute squeezes, they may threaten a more ruthless pruning of their existing operations.

What is striking about most of the period after 1960 is that the rate of investment was maintained at a higher level than in the 1950s. There seem two types of explanation for this. The first is that though it was falling, the level of profit continued to provide adequate incentive to invest; it might indeed be argued that the increased competition made investment seem more necessary, provided it was sufficiently profitable. The second type of explanation is more subjective: the increased level of government incentives were attractive on the one hand; while some of the factors reducing real profitability were either not noticed, because inflation was not taken properly into account, or were, when older investment had to be written off faster than expected, thought to be once-for-all misfortunes.

These explanations are, perhaps, too much in terms of entrepreneurial expectations. The function of profits in a capitalistic economy is twofold: expectation of them provides an incentive to invest; and their receipt provides finance for investment. This picture is modified by the existence of external finance; and it was an important factor in the post-war world, as compared with the 1930s, that large supplies of funds became available from institutional sources, and that, once expectations of permanent inflation became general, many of these were willing to buy equities at prices which seemed to managers to represent low cost financing. Nevertheless, generally, external finance could only expand on a base of achieved profits and accumulated capital. Companies that borrowed, as companies generally did in the 1960s, and accumulated debt faster than their profits rose, were following a policy that could not be persisted in indefinitely.

The actual end of the boom in 1974 had a fortuitous cause. During the fifties and sixties when some restraint had been placed on credit by directions to the commercial banks, many quasi-banking institutions had grown up to take advantage of the opportunities which the banks were unable to exploit. A drastic reform of the credit system by the Bank of England's edict 'Competition and Credit Control' (1971) removed many of the banks' comparative handicaps, and from then on the scope for other institutions was narrowed. But this effect was disguised by an undisciplined expansion of credit to which bad management of the new system gave rise. Rather like its predecessor in 1844, the Bank assumed that the new system would automatically deal with all problems. In fact it led to the most serious financial crisis in Britain since 1866; share prices fell by a larger proportion than ever before; many institutions had to be rescued by the banking system under the leadership of the Bank of England; and all institutions had drastically to revise the lax assumptions about the low risks of borrowing that had accumulated during the previous thirty years.

The circumstances of 1974, a credit crisis of a kind unprecedented in living memory, and the effects of galloping wage inflation on the liquidity of all firms, brought the boom of 1972–4, and indeed the longer investment boom of the sixties and early seventies, to an end. (Investment in North Sea oil masked the extent of this decline in the aggregate statistics.)

How much importance should be attached to the events of 1973–4? Were they of importance in themselves or did they just make more abrupt and obvious a change in climate that would have come in any case? For a country like the U.K., inextricably involved in the international economy, not to be able to cope with changes in the terms of trade is a symptom of the inflexibility of its institutions and the unreality of the expectations of either the work-force or the electorate. Nevertheless, it must be accepted that the extent and abruptness of the rise in oil prices, together with the monetary effects of the inability of the oil states to spend their revenue, was an exceptional disturbance. But more importance could be attached to it in the case of the U.K. were it not for the equally exceptional, nearly coincident and wholly fortuitous, good fortune of North Sea oil.

The actual course of inflation in 1974 and '75, in which earnings raced ahead of prices, perhaps augmenting rather than relieving feelings of relative injustice, coming after several years in which the particular form of prices and incomes policies adopted had eroded profitability, brought the economy into deep crisis. It has been argued here that the events of those years aggravated trends that were already apparent: in profitability and in the decline of the growth of employment. Yet the point at which profitability fell to a critical level cannot be judged with any precision (who knows whether five or eight per cent is an adequate real return on capital?). Again, it is worth remembering that, while between 1966 and 1971 the working population declined by half a million, between

1971 and 1976 it increased by 950,000 and that this, rather than exceptional lack of growth of opportunities, may explain most of the increase in unemployment.

In short, whether the crises of the later seventies are better seen as the culmination of longer trends precipitated by the events of 1973–5, or whether they were so considerably aggravated as to be effectively caused by those events is an unresolved, and perhaps an unresolvable, question.

It has not been possible to escape and observe the period entirely detached from the preoccupations of the seventies. Consequently it is a lugubrious tale. This itself may be a phenomenon of the times. The almost continuous discussion associated with government management of the economy in a democracy has led to a devaluation of language in describing sacrifices and privations and blameworthiness. Economists must share the responsibility as practitioners of an approach that tends to set standards of indefinite perfectibility; so that, if imperfections are not perceptible at one level of magnification, the lens moves more closely until the imperfection occupies a sizeable part of the screen.

Measured straightforwardly in material terms, there has been a considerable improvement for almost everyone in Britain in the middle third of the twentieth century; and the setbacks experienced have involved hardships that are small when set against those of industrialized economies of the nineteenth century or those produced by natural disasters in less developed parts of the world today, and completely trivial in comparison with the effects of war or natural disaster in earlier times.

Suggestions for reading

A short list

R. S. Sayers, *A History of Economic Change in England 1880–1939* (Oxford, 1967) provides a general account of Britain in the preceding period. S. Pollard, *The Development of the British Economy 1914–67* (2nd edition, Arnold, 1969) provides a summary of events and a review of literature for the period up to 1967 that is thorough and detailed. The National Institute of Economic and Social Research, *The United Kingdom Economy* (2nd edition, Heineman, 1976) provides a description of the U.K. in the 1970s which contains succinct summaries of many aspects of post-war developments. G. C. Allen, *British Industries and their Organization* (Fifth edition, Longman, 1970) provides detail on the development of individual industries both during the period and in the previous fifty years.

A fuller list

All the above should be accessible to non-economists. The same warranty cannot be given about all the following, though most contain little or no highly technical material.

General

A. K. Cairncross; 'The Post-War Years 1945–75' in R. Floud & D. N. McCloskey (eds.), *The New Economic History of the U.K.* (Cambridge, forthcoming) provides a succinct summary by a distinguished economic historian who was also involved almost continuously as an economic adviser. G. A. Phillips & R. T. Maddock, *The Growth of the British Economy 1918–1968* (Allen & Unwin, 1973) is a not very technical economic analysis; A. Peaker, *Economic Growth in Modern Britain* (Macmillan, 1974) is made slightly more difficult for non-economists by its brevity.

Economic management

Most of the period is covered by a succession of more detailed works concerned with government policy in the medium period: W. K. Hancock & M. M. Gowing, *British War Economy* (H.M.S.O., 1949); G. D. N. Worswick & P. Ady (eds.), *The British Economy 1945–50* (Oxford, 1952); G. D. N. Worswick & P. Ady (eds.), *The British Economy in the 1950s* (Oxford, 1962); F. T. Blackaby (ed.), *British Economic Policy 1960–74* (Cambridge, 1978); and one over a slightly shorter period: W. Beckerman, *The Labour Government's Economic Record 1964–1970* (Duckworth, 1972).

R. E. Caves and associates, *Britain's Economic Prospects* (Allen & Unwin, 1968) and A. Cairncross, (ed.), *Britain's Economic Prospects Reconsidered* (Allen & Unwin, 1970) contain many contributions that looked some way back into Britain's economic development. S. Brittan, *Steering the Economy* (Penguin, 1970) is a lively account of the previous twenty years, as is M. Stewart, *Politics and Economic Policy in the U.K. since 1964* (Pergamon, 1978). D. Winch, *Economics and Policy* (Fontana, 1969) provides a clear, if optimistic, survey of the influence of economic theory on policy. A. Budd, *The Politics of Economic Planning* (Fontana, 1978) provides a fairly brief résumé of the history of economic planning in the U.K. D. N. Chester (ed.), *Lessons of the British War Economy* (Cambridge, 1951) provides illuminating views of certain aspects of the management of the Second World War. William Beveridge, *Full Employment in a Free Society* (Allen and Unwin, 1944) is a historical document in its own right.

Some other suggestions

J. H. Dunning & C. J. Thomas, *British Industry* (Hutchinson, 1963) provides some detail on technical change. C. F. Pratten, 'The Reasons for the Slow Economic Progress of the British Economy' in *Oxford Economic Papers* (July 1972) provides a more detailed analysis of the economies of growth and scale in modern industry. C. F. Pratten, *Labour Productivity Differentials Within International Companies* (Cambridge, 1976) is in the nature of a 'controlled' experiment, comparing British and foreign labour working under the same management. K. Norris and J. Vaizey, *The Economics of Research and Technology* (Allen & Unwin, 1973) provides a good survey, though it is not specifically historical. L. Hannah, *The Rise of the Corporate Economy* (Methuen, 1976) provides a long perspective and a thorough account of the changes in company organization and the effects of mergers. K. D. George, *Industrial Organization* (2nd edition, Allen & Unwin, 1974) provides an excellent summary of the developments of the period in the organization of industry. G. Routh, *Occupation and Pay in Britain 1906–60* (Cambridge, 1965) provides a long-term review of pay differentials and occupational distribution up to 1960. Unfortunately there does not exist an *economic* history of labour in the U.K. for the more recent period. Henry Phelps Brown, *The Inequality of Pay* (Oxford, 1977), though not specifically historical, includes some relevant material.

Appendix: statistical sources

The following works, which are recommended to the reader for further reference, have provided the data on which the figures and tables of the book are based. All publications listed below are published by Her Majesty's Stationary Office unless otherwise stated.

By far the most useful single recommendation I can make is:

1 London and Cambridge Economic Service, *The British Economy Key Statistics 1900–1970* (Times Newspapers, 1972)

Some of its series can be continued after 1970 in:

2 Central Statistical Office, *Economic Trends Annual Supplement*

Others are continued in:

3 Central Statistical Office, *Annual Abstract of Statistics*, which also contains many other series of interest.

An alternative to 1 which is less compactly arranged but has a wider range of data for the period to 1965 is:

4 B. R. Mitchell & H. G. Jones, *Second Abstract of British Historical Statistics* (Cambridge, 1971)

which continues:

5 B. R. Mitchell & P. Deane, *Abstract of British Historical Statistics*, (Cambridge, 1962)

though this is primarily of use for the preceding period.

1 and 2 provide a good many national income data, but some components have to be extracted from:

6 Central Statistical Office, *National Income and Expenditure* (Annual) and

7 Central Statistical Office, *United Kingdom Balance of Payments* (Annual), of which the key issue is 1971, which contains series for the whole period since 1946.

National income estimates for a much longer period are to be found in:

8   C. H. Feinstein, *National Income Expenditure and Output 1855–1965*, (Cambridge, 1972).

Much data on incomes and employment is contained in:

9   Department of Employment, *British Labour Statistics Historical Abstract 1886–1968*, which is brought up to date by *British Labour Statistics Yearbook* (Annual).

10   C.S.O., *Social Trends* (Annual)
provides much relevant information on consumption, employment, and income distribution. Unfortunately most of its information does not extend over long periods.

11   The Royal Commission on the Distribution of Income and Wealth has since 1974 provided new information. Much of this relates to the 1970s, but the Reports do contain the best available historical series. See particularly:
The Initial Report on the Standing Reference (Cmnd 6171).

12   R. C. O. Matthews, C. H. Feinstein and J. Odling-Smee, *British Economic Growth in Historical Perspective* when published will contain authoritative discussion, and many calculations and estimates.

Index